RECONSTRUCTING THE RUBBLE

Praise for *Reconstructing the Rubble*

"A very timely topic, Kevin Jack handles it with care and practicality. So many people today are rethinking their faith. This book is a reminder that thinking can play a huge role in our faith, and that we can end up on the other side of reconstruction with a faith still in tact."

—**Dr. Tim Elmore**, CEO of <u>GrowingLeaders.com</u>

"Years ago, I wrote the book, *Toxic Faith* which helped people identify authentic Christianity from the destructive counterfeits of that era. Now, Pastor Kevin Jack has written a contemporary book on the devastating effect that the deconstructing of our faith is having on believers and those who are searching for God. Even more importantly, Kevin provides a solid plan and the Godly path developing a stronger faith if you have been left without it or your faith has been severely weakened. *Reconstructing the Rubble* is a powerful and timely book that will build and strengthen your faith and help you impact others as they struggle during this difficult time."

Stephen Arterburn is a best-selling author with over 12,000,000 books in print and hosts the daily "New Life Live" radio program. Steve is also the *Teaching Pastor* at the 3rd Fastest Growing Church in America, Northview Church in Carmel, Indiana where he and his family reside. He can be reached at <u>SArterburn@newlife.com</u>.

In a world longing for something permanent but lacking a biblical imagination, it is easy to become cynical and lose hope. Kevin Jack is a pastor who understands the existential questions without providing simplistic answers. Drawing from his experience of leading churches that reach many who have given up on religion, Kevin offers a refreshing return to the beliefs and practices of a faith centered on Jesus. This feels like a right-on-time resource for ministry in the secular age."

—**David Busic**, General Superintendent
Church of the Nazarene"

"In *Reconstructing the Rubble* Kevin has expertly navigated a difficult topic that I have grappled with both personally and professionally throughout my years in ministry. This book identifies really important principles that will equip you for the difficult journey of helping people rebuild their faith when it has been broken. If you are leading people in ministry, read this book!"

— **Tim Fisher**, Pastor of
Crossroads Community Church

"I love Kevin Jack and I love how he combines self-exposing humor with his own life experiences to make biblical faith accessible and applicable to people at all levels of understanding. This book is full of real-life illustrations of how to learn to live, with an informed measure of faith, while still hanging on to your brain. Enjoy!"

— **Brett Rickey**
Pastor of Highland Park Church

"Author of *Stay in the Yard, Chasing Cool, Boomerang: The Return of the Prodigal Son,* Kevin Jack is a pastor, leader, and writer for this generation and generations to come. He offers a fresh and creative way to examine the true life of faith through the process of *Reconstructing the Rubble.* You will be encouraged and challenged as you journey through the pages of this book to not just have more faith, but to understand, to build, and to live faith."

— **Selena Freeman**, Lead Pastor, The Well Church

"For decades the culture has been on a quest to seek truth and a deeper way of living. Since the 1960's every generation has asked hard questions and very often found their religion of birth lacking. Astonishingly, there are few road maps to a meaningful exploration of faith, truth and Christians thought. Kevin Jacks offers one of the first and most comprehensive guidebooks to the search for meaning. That it comes from an author who has lived the journey of his generations search, makes this book immensely valuable to those on the journey and others who are attempting to support them in their search!"

— **Dave Roberts,** Pastor of Montrose Church,
Author of Healing Conversations

RECONSTRUCTING
THE RUBBLE

*REBUILDING YOUR FAITH EVEN WHEN
YOU'RE UNSURE HOW IT FELL APART*

KEVIN JACK

NASHVILLE

NEW YORK • LONDON • MELBOURNE • VANCOUVER

RECONSTRUCTING THE RUBBLE
REBUILDING YOUR FAITH EVEN WHEN
YOU'RE UNSURE HOW IT FELL APART

Published in New York, New York, by Morgan James Publishing. Morgan James is a trademark of Morgan James, LLC. www.MorganJamesPublishing.com

Unless otherwise noted, Scriptures taken from the Holy Bible, New International Version®, NIV®.

Copyright © 1973, 1978, 1984, 2011 by Biblica, Inc.™

Used by permission of Zondervan. All rights reserved worldwide.

www.zondervan.com

The "NIV" and "New International Version" are trademarks registered in the United States Patent and Trademark Office by Biblica, Inc.™

ISBN 978-1-63195-165-7 paperback
ISBN 978-1-63195-166-4 eBook
Library of Congress Control Number: 2020911148

Morgan James is a proud partner of Habitat for Humanity Peninsula and Greater Williamsburg. Partners in building since 2006.

Get involved today! Visit
www.MorganJamesBuilds.com

To Madi, Emmy, Molly, and Parker.
May your faith be stretched
and grow stronger every day.

TABLE OF CONTENTS

INTRODUCTION

My friends left the church.

I made new friends (thanks for asking), and I'm fairly introverted so I don't need that many friends anyway. Four, maybe five, would be just fine. This isn't a cry for help. It's not a passive-aggressive second request for an RSVP to the party because I'm afraid no one is going to show up, like when I was seven. This is far more important than that.

This is a life-ring thrown overboard for anyone who wants to grab hold. Some people won't want to; they'd rather tread water. I get exhausted treading water.

You see, many of my friends left the church. While I absolutely want them back, the reality is they, too, want to come back. They just don't know how. And while they long for a faith that's real, they're not exactly sure why they should come back.

Like many of us, they have memories—both positive and negative—from their time in the church. There are joys, and there are also scars, but it's not the scars that are keeping them away. I tore my knee open when I was thrown off my bike at age eight. I still have that scar today, and I still ride my bike.

It's not the scars that keep people away. It's that our faith has been disassembled. The previously built foundation of belief has been removed. Sometimes, piece-by-piece. Sometimes, crashing down all at once. Often, we didn't even realize it was happening.

Some of that disassembly is incredibly important. Often our childish faith is filled with false beliefs, half-truths, and poor theology. When that weak foundation is only asked to support the light load of childhood, it works just fine. But when that childish foundation is asked to withstand the pressures of being an adult, it begins to crack . . . and eventually collapse. The foundation that can support a fisher-price house cannot support a mansion. To be stable, these pieces need to be taken apart and the understructure replaced with a more sturdy foundation.

We do this with beliefs all the time. When I was a kid, I believed in Santa (if you still do . . . stop reading, like right now). When I discovered there was no Santa (warned you), I didn't simply discard the belief. I replaced it with a stronger belief. I am now more grateful to my parents for what they did for my sisters and myself. A childish expectation was replaced with an adult belief.

But here's the problem: For many of us, the foundation was never upgraded. We took apart the pieces of our faith and never filled the gaps with something stronger. We disassembled our faith and then never built again.

This is a call to build again.

For those whose faith has become nothing more than a pile of rubble, I want to help you reconstruct it. And for those who have seen someone whose faith has been disassembled, I believe you can help them find a stronger faith. One that is transformative. One that is defining. A faith that calls us deeper than we would normally go and stretches us beyond anything we would have ventured into on our own. A faith that truly matters.

I believe in the depths of my heart that faith in Jesus changes everything. That's what I want for you. Let's get to work.

CHAPTER ONE

ADULT LEGOS

I didn't realize there was a controversy over Legos, not until I saw *The Lego Movie*.

If you have yet to experience the privilege of watching this cinematic masterpiece (that was a bit overstated), *The Lego Movie's* plot revolves around the question, "Should Legos be built however you want, or should they be carefully constructed based upon the instructions and then locked into place?"

I loved Legos. I "loved," as in used to—past tense. Now my love for them has been severely impeded by the fact that my most common interaction with Legos is stepping on them with my bare foot. It's hard to love someone or something when the only time you get together they stab you in the heel. Such is my relationship with Legos.

As a kid, I didn't have any Lego "sets." My friends would talk about building the Millennium Falcon or the Eiffel Tower, but I had no idea what that was like. My Lego "sets" were someone else's "set," usually missing half the pieces because we had collected them at garage sales and then threw them all together in an enormous bin. All I knew was building whatever you wanted to build.

It wasn't until my children became intrigued by Legos that I learned how to build a Lego set properly. While I assumed that IKEA furniture would be proper training, I came to realize that my furniture assembly hubris would be my downfall. What should have been a simple exercise in putting together Rapunzel's tower (I've got three girls), turned out to be an incredibly frustrating venture. It's not that I was overmatched. In the end, I succeeded. The problem was I didn't realize how similar some of the pieces were. So I would put a piece in place, only to realize four steps later that the piece I had recently used was actually needed in another place. I would have to disassemble what I was building and go back to build it the right way.

I'm not attempting to be overdramatic, but every time I had to disassemble, I wanted to quit. Just for a moment, I had to remind myself why I needed to keep going. This wasn't difficult since three girls were anxiously awaiting the completion of their tower. But every time I had to disassemble, it took an act of the will to go back and build again.

It was so frustrating to know that I could've been further along, and I had to go back and fix the mistakes I had made, over and over. I could've kept going, but the pieces that were supposed to be in place were necessary for the stability of the tower. If I just put the pieces in the wrong places, the tower would've crumbled. Even when I was annoyed because I had to deconstruct the tower, I had to choose to keep building.

Somewhere within our faith, we quit building.

We gave up. We called it quits. We pulled so many pieces off that we were left with nothing, and we decided to be done.

This is what deconstruction has done within many of our faiths; it's become a pile of rubble. Nothing more than scattered Legos thrown into a bin. All the pieces are there, but it's not really in a condition for us to see anything worthwhile.

Understanding Deconstruction

Think of deconstruction like putting together a Lego set. There is a proper way for it to be held together. If the set is going to do what it was created to do, then there is a way in which it must be constructed. We acknowledge that faith is different in one respect: There are many different ways for our beliefs to be constructed in a healthy way. There is not "one exact way" for people to come to a place of belief.

But just because there are many good options for how to believe and come to a place of belief, it doesn't mean there aren't also some bad options. Just because there isn't one *correct* way, doesn't mean there aren't also *incorrect* ways. I could refer to a horse by a multitude of names—a colt, a foal, a mare, a stallion, or a mustang—and I may be right. But if I called a horse a donkey, I would be wrong. (Full disclosure: I know nothing about horses. I had to Google all of that, even to make sure a donkey wasn't some sort of a weird mini horse.)

Everyone's faith must be deconstructed at various points throughout their lives. We don't take a straight path into maturity. We stumble, we struggle, we wander, and we move forward. Deconstruction is part of maturity.

This happens most commonly in three specific ways:

1. When significant experiences or moments make us reconsider what we once were so sure was undeniably true.

These moments come any time an experience contrasts with a belief. We prayed and were convinced that God would answer, but He didn't . . . at least not the way we expected Him to. All of a sudden, the belief, "God always answers prayer," needs to be deconstructed because of our experience. Some people throw away prayer all together, while others will allow for that deconstruction to lead to a healthier belief: God always answers prayer, but the answer can be yes, no, or wait.

If you are a fundamentalist then this type of moment becomes the death sentence on your faith. Fundamentalists believe everyone must have a faith that is just like them. Others must behave how they behave, believe exactly what they believe, and come to belief through a similar experience as they did. I've seen two, and only two, outcomes for these kinds of people. 1) They are exhausted by the weight of their fundamentalist policing behavior. They still hold on to their beliefs, but it becomes far more of a weight than a joy; and 2) As soon as any bit of doubt creeps in, their beliefs come toppling down. Instead of continuously rethinking their beliefs based upon a firm, sturdy foundation, their belief system functions like a contraption where if one screw is loose, the whole thing falls apart. The doubt most commonly creeps in when an experience comes in contrast with a belief. Questions about evil, suffering, and how the power of God interacts with free will may be examples.

2. When our perspectives have been broadened and we have to hold together the possibility that two seemingly opposed ideas can now fit together.

When I was younger I was taught that drinking alcohol is wrong. Not bad, not unhelpful, not possibly harmful, but wrong. We didn't talk about Jesus turning water into wine;

it was more like Kool-Aid (you know, because everyone thinks the best wine tastes like Kool-Aid). I am sure the influence of this teaching is partially the reason why, to this day I have never had anything stronger than cough syrup to drink. Humorously, there was a time when that fact would have been met with affirmation. Now it is most commonly met with shock and derision. (That's fine. I don't need your approval!)

This teaching—my truth—became hard for me to understand when many of my Christian friends drank. I thought, "How could they? Don't they know what the Bible says about alcohol?" I promptly made new friends who didn't drink. (Apparently, I make a fantastic Pharisee!) Over time, I met people whom I respected only to later discover they regularly consumed alcohol. All of a sudden, I had two ideas, and both couldn't be true: 1) Drinking alcohol is morally wrong and 2) This person who drinks is a moral, loving, kind follower of Christ who has integrity. This forced me to investigate what the Bible said about alcohol, and I learned it does not say drinking is morally wrong! Being open to new perspectives forced me to deconstruct and reconsider beliefs, ones I once thought couldn't fit together. We often assume that issues of political affiliation, denominational beliefs, and practices that are specific to our tribe are dictated in scripture, only to find out faith is broader than that. (Side Note: I still don't drink, and I'm actually a huge fan of Kool-Aid.)

3. When we grow up and we have to replace our childhood beliefs with adult ideas.

Think back through the math classes you had growing up (I'm sorry to do this to you). In Kindergarten, we were taught two specific things: 1) The higher up the numbers go, the greater the value and 2) Letters and numbers are separate. I can vividly remember my teacher attempting to switch our brains from Math to Language Arts. We had done our work with numbers, now it was time to put them away so "the Letter people" could come out. They were always separate.

Because of this teaching method, I can remember my brain being blown at two specific moments, with negative numbers and algebra. Go back to your young self. You knew ten was more than seven. It was so simple to understand that having ten of something was better than having seven of something. Then, all of a sudden, teachers put that stupid little line in front of the number, and it meant that it was reversed! -10 became less than -7. Craziness! Then a couple years later, math problems included letters! Absurd! The teaching that helped me understand a concept at an elementary level had to be abandoned. If I was going to continue to grow to a higher level of understanding in math I had to reconsider prior beliefs to gain advanced concepts.

The three examples above are the most common contexts for deconstruction to take place. All three are necessary and important. No one would simply add a third level to a two-story house blueprint. We understand that if we are going to add another floor to our house, we would need to upgrade the foundation. (I'm sure you have to do other stuff as well, I know nothing about construction.) If I'm going to increase the load that a structure is attempting to carry, I need to increase the strength of the structure. Our childish faith was not meant to be handle the weight of sickness, disasters, mass shootings, feelings of purposelessness, mental illness, loss . . . the list could go on forever. What we were taught throughout Sunday School, kids church, VBS, camp, Veggie Tales movies, or whatever else on Earth was used was always meant to be deconstructed and built upon later. Deconstruction is healthy when it is done in the areas of our faith that need to be rebuilt.

This is where the problem comes in. Unlike with my kids' Lego sets, we don't have an instruction manual for our faith. I know what you're thinking, "But what about the Bible! Doesn't it stand for **B**asic **I**nstructions **B**efore **L**eaving **E**arth!" to which I would say, "Come on. Like seriously, come on!" If the Bible is written as an instruction manual, I wholeheartedly take back everything I said about the geniuses at IKEA and Lego, whom I now realize make their instructions impeccably clear and so unbelievably simple to understand. I repent, and those Swedish furniture wizards have my apologies.

To make sure we are clear on the idea that the Bible is not an instruction manual, allow me a brief exploration of what would happen if we treated Scripture that way. An instruction manual is a step-by-step guide to build something. So if we were to start with Scripture, we would begin with: 1) God created in seven days 2) Don't eat fruit that you're not supposed to, and 3) Don't kill your brother. While all points are helpful pieces of advice, I ask, "Where within those is the helpful piece in understanding how to build my faith?" I can think of no one who, in seeking to disciple a new believer, started the process with a lecture on creation, proper fruit eating, and a word of caution against homicide. Now some may say, "You're starting at the wrong place; you should start in Matthew or John." So you're telling me that I should start two-thirds of the way through the instruction manual? Super helpful (commence sarcastic slow clap)!"

We'll get to the importance of Scripture within building our faith at a later chapter, but for now, let's settle on this point: The Bible is not a step-by-step guide for knowing how to build your faith. And if the Bible isn't an instruction manual, then the reality is, there isn't one. Let that set in for a second. While there are guides, aids, role models, teachings, and the unbelievable power of the spirit of God, there isn't a specific instruction manual for building faith, which means, when our faith is being deconstructed, it isn't obvious where to stop.

Let's think through the moment you realize you put a Lego piece in the wrong place in the set. Once you come to the realization that something doesn't fit, your first step is to go back through the instructions and see where the error was made. Then you begin disassembling the set until you reach the spot where you made the error, *and you go no further*. You wouldn't get two-thirds of the way through the creation, realize you made an error on Step 18, and then promptly smash the entire set so you could start all over. (Side note: If you do that, you may need a counselor.) No, you begin taking the pieces apart until you get back to the error so the structure can be stronger . . . so it can be better.

The point I want to make is that our faith does not provide us with a step-by-step instruction manual. As a result, when we begin deconstructing our faith, it isn't obvious where to stop. Simple questions that should cause us to reconsider one aspect of our theology, or one piece of how we've been living our lives, sometimes result in some of us tearing apart everything that has been built. And then throwing away the foundation.

Here's a common example. Recorded in Mark 11:23, Jesus says, "Truly I tell you, if anyone says to this mountain, 'Go throw yourself into the sea,' and does not doubt in their heart but believes that what they say will happen, it will be done for them." Now, I've never had that happen, have you? I've prayed for many things and believed in many things, but I have not often had anything tangible happen because of it. A seed of doubt is planted deep within our faith. We begin to think, "If Jesus said that, and I've never had that happen, then maybe the other things he said weren't true either."

If there were an instruction manual, we would relook at our understanding of Mark 11:23 and assess what Jesus truly meant through that statement. But instead of replacing a wrong belief with a right belief, we begin dismantling everything that has been built.

To switch metaphors—years ago I put together a piece of furniture, and the instructions were unbelievably unclear. As if these sub-par cave paintings weren't difficult enough, my problem was aided by the fact that the manufacturer did not include enough of certain pieces and too many of others. I had to go out and purchase a new set of screws and had four washers left over. (I know what you're thinking.)

As I was going through the assembly, I became increasingly frustrated about how unclear the directions were and about having to disassemble the set. However over time, I was able to create checkpoints. I was able to create some natural spots in which I knew I had assembled the piece correctly. Every time something didn't work, I looked back at the instructions to this point because I knew everything before that point was assembled correctly. That step became an anchor for my assembly.

While we don't have an instruction manual, our faith badly needs anchors, natural checkpoints for us to come back to. These are safe places we know, where we don't need to deconstruct beyond this point.

That's what I want to explore with you. I want to help you find some natural spots you can continuously go back to. I want you to be able to find your own foundational points so that as you continue to deconstruct, you don't have to unnecessarily start all over. But first we need to do some foundational work. Because the reality is many people reading this have, or know people who have, deconstructed their faith all the way to nothing. We need to know what to do with the empty Lego set and we need to know how we got there.

CHAPTER TWO

SOMEONE TOOK
OFF THEIR GLASSES

My future wife and I were out on a date, and it was going terribly. We didn't do many creative dates; we were pretty happy just hanging out with each other. On this particular date in college, we had driven an hour to the closest mall (that was worth hanging out at). And I was bored. Really bored. I'm not always smart (understatement), so throughout the night, I repeatedly asked Bethany if she was bored as well. She said no. I continued to ask her about every twenty minutes. She continued to say no. This went on for about two hours. It's amazing we're married today.

If we'd just started dating, I'm fairly certain this date would've felt like the end of the relationship. But we'd been dating for a little over three years at the time and knew how to survive a horrific date, no matter how boring it was. As we were driving back to campus, I asked her again if she was bored. This time, she didn't answer but began to question me about what "on Earth" was wrong. I'd like to say it was a very gentle, compassionate method of questioning, but that's not really how we roll.

Then it dawned on her. Her expression changed, and she began to laugh. I had no idea what was going on. It was then she reminded me that as we were on our way to the mall, my allergies had been bothering me (because I'm allergic to everything in the world), and she had given me two Benadryl. I almost never take any medication because my body doesn't handle medication well. (I'm sure that fact, in addition to the previous admission of allergies, is helping you see how truly masculine I am!) As an example, a couple of years later, when I needed surgery for a broken nose, they gave me anesthesia, and I promptly quit breathing altogether. Like I said, my body doesn't handle medication well. Giving me two Benadryl pills is like giving a normal person an elephant tranquilizer. With this information, we were able to laugh about how the night had gone. While Bethany was having a good time, I was barely awake. I wasn't bored; I was drugged.

Our perspectives were entirely different. As we laughed, I pulled over, we switched drivers, and then I took a nap for the rest of the way home.

In sixth grade, we learned about worldviews. We learned about different religions, and we learned about how someone's background will influence how they see things. We learned about how ethnicity, economic stability, childhood trauma, and everything else in someone's life will impact their perspective. The point of the lesson was simple; everyone has a worldview. Your worldview, quite literally, changes how you see the world.

When I put on sunglasses, I see the world differently. When I take Benadryl, I see dates differently. When I read without glasses, I see the words differently (poorly). Everything we do and everything that has happened to us impacts the way we see the world. We each have a unique set of glasses we wear, and those glasses are formed by our backgrounds, beliefs, experiences, and desires, which all impact how we see the world.

This lesson is incredibly important. It explains both why I got into fights with my sisters and why the Middle East has been in conflict for centuries. We don't see things the same way. Within this idea is a humbling truth: We are all subjective. Every one of us has unique experiences, backgrounds, and beliefs that give us a unique perspective on the world. We interpret events differently, we respond to different types of problems, and we have certain reactions that come more naturally. We all have a unique pair of glasses that colors how we see the world.

In the book *Hillbilly Elegy*, JD Vance describes the glasses that someone with a white Appalachian background might wear. In his amazing account, he describes why people from that part of the world, with that background, have a specific way of responding to conflict, responding to authority, and even spending money. The point is simple: When this is your worldview, your actions make sense. What may seem absurd to others makes perfect sense to you.

What we're acknowledging is that we each have a unique lens with which we see the world. Our beliefs, backgrounds, relationships, life experiences, family dynamics . . . let me make it simple—*everything* about us shapes this lens. Experiences that your grandparents had shapes your lens through the culture of your family. We're each subjective, meaning we each carry biases in some form or fashion.

This understanding seems simple, but it's incredibly important. The humility to acknowledge that we have a subjective lens with which we see the world has enabled us to understand the perspective of someone who may see things more clearly than we do. The lack of humility to acknowledge our subjective lens leads to bigotry. It believes, "If everyone would just see the world how I see it then everything would be right." The essence of that lack of humility is seen in people who will acknowledge that oppression has been something people have experienced since the creation of the world, but who cannot acknowledge that oppression for some people is a reality today. (Side note: Never ask the people who might be guilty of oppressing others if there is oppression in the world today. They never think there's a problem.)

This is where we've lived for a while. We understand that everyone has a unique perspective, we all have a pair of glasses that uniquely shapes how we see the world. We need humility to acknowledge our subjectivity, and that humility enables us to learn from one another and to grow.

Now here's the problem: somewhere over the last couple of decades we've abandoned this idea.

Not everyone. Not for everything. Only specifically when it comes to religious beliefs.

We now think some people don't wear glasses.

For a multitude of reasons we now live in a world in which we assume that everyone's perspective is subjective *except* when it comes to the arena of our faith. And here is the new mentality: You are subjective *unless* you are an atheist. If you have no belief in God then you are objective. If you do not have belief in a higher power, you no longer have a perspective. You are now seeing things clearly, objectively.

We believe that those who don't believe in a higher power have "the" worldview rather than "a" worldview. They took their glasses off while the rest of us are stuck seeing with our tainted perspectives.

Not that long ago, it was considered important for a political candidate to claim allegiance to some higher deity. I understand there are roots within this thought system, which are phenomenally unhealthy, but for the purpose of this discussion, let's look briefly at the healthy side. A belief in a higher power by an elected official was considered a sign of strength, that their morality was rooted in something deeper than their feelings and their humility was intact. We associated a deeper level of trust with these politicians because of their beliefs on the origins of right and wrong and the eternal implications that are associated with our actions.

This is no longer the case. Now, we're highly concerned about a candidate who appears to be "super-religious." We fear their beliefs might reduce their objectivity.

For most of us, we have bought into this mentality so strongly that we don't push back at all. And this is what we're saying: People with a worldview that maintains a belief in a deity are too compromised to be in a prominent role because they no longer have sound reasoning. But someone with a worldview that doesn't include a deity can be trusted because they are objective in their reasoning.

There's a beautiful fable written by Hans Christian Andersen that illustrates what has happened. In "The Emperor's New Clothes," we find the story of out-of-town tailors who promise to make the emperor beautiful, new clothes that anyone who is intelligent can see. You know how the story goes. There are no clothes, but no one will admit it for risk of being called a fool. This continues until, as the emperor is being paraded through the town, a child states, "But he hasn't got anything on!" This creates a ripple effect where now everyone is willing to admit that the emperor, indeed, is naked.

I was taught everyone has a worldview, that everyone is subjective. This doesn't mean everyone is right. It means everyone is a little wrong. For Christians, we believe Jesus is objective. We believe Jesus provides the only true, correct lens through which to see the world, but our opinion of him, our understanding of him, is subjective. As Paul writes, "Now we see in a mirror dimly. . ." our perspective is skewed.

While this is still true, we no longer believe that. In "The Emperor's New Clothes," the emperor claimed to have clothes when he had none, and if you disagreed with him, you were labeled unusually stupid. The modern-day humanists posture themselves as if they aren't wearing glasses, as if they don't have a worldview. Like the fable, if you disagree with them, you are labeled a fool.

Typically, in a work like this, we would now try to prove that we are all indeed subjective. That everyone has a worldview. To do that we would:

1. Show that our current philosophy did not come out of nowhere. This philosophy is not like an alien arriving from another planet. We would show the progression it took to get to this point and how each step has been subjective (and often with an agenda)

to show that you cannot arrive at an objective reality through a subjective path.

2. Expose the holes in this philosophy by simply pointing out the arrogance that is required for it. To do that, we'd look at errors in science and thought processes through recent history and show the hubris it would take to actually believe, "Yes, science and research made errors in their conclusions in the past, but we no longer do that."

3. Show examples of the exceptions to this "objective view." And how we are often faced with data that cannot be explained (often referred to as miracles), and how the secular community has had to bend-over-backwards to attempt to keep their views intact so they can still feel in control.

That's what we would do, but I'll leave that work for a different author. Someone better equipped to take on those arguments. I find another piece far more fascinating. It's looking at the world that this view will create. What would the world really look like, if there was no faith, no belief. If all that existed was the secular worldview, what would life look like?

That's the discussion we'll turn to in the next chapter, the realities of the empty Lego set.

CHAPTER THREE

THE EMPTY LEGO SET

We live in a world significantly impacted by the Christian faith. We can argue whether that has been good or bad, but either way, the echoes of the Christian faith can be heard all over the globe. Christianity has shifted the world with regards to our language, our values, and even our infrastructure.

I don't want to belabor this point, but I do want to make sure we're on the same page. If I say, "The presence of TV contracts has changed professional sports," I'm not saying that TV contracts are good or bad. You could argue that it has made the games more entertaining to watch and has increased enjoyment because of that participation; or you could argue that it has diluted the quality of play and has resulted in rule changes that are better for the fans but not for the competitive nature of the sport. We're not saying that it's good or bad but simply, that it has made an impact. If I say, "Digital platforms have revolutionized the music world," you may stand on the side that the revolution has been a good thing because it's made music accessible to people who wouldn't have previously had access and has enabled artists to become part of a global music scene they would have never had before; or you may stand on the side that says the revolution has been bad, and we've made it almost impossible for all but a few select artists to make a living by cultivating their craft. We can disagree on whether the impact is good or bad, but it should not be difficult to agree that an impact has been made.

Whether you are a professing Christian, a staunch atheist, or an apathetic bystander (who I doubt is reading this book. You know, because of the apathy . . .) the statement, "The world has been significantly impacted by the Christian faith" should be something we can easily agree on. At this point, we might get into an argument as to whether that impact has been good or bad. So we talk about hospitals and crusades; the Salem witch trials and literacy; missionaries as colonization and medical missionaries as a refuge; the inquisition and everything else.

Rather than have the argument that many of us have had in coffee shops, over awkward meals at Thanksgiving, or in college lecture halls, I want to ask a new question. "What would the world look like today if it was rid of the influence of Christianity?"

This is the piece of deconstruction no one seems to talk about, but that I believe essential. But first, we need to acknowledge something . . .

My kids love to build Lego sets. But there is one thing they love even more than building their creations. They love to tear down the creations of their siblings. This may be a deep incrimination on my parenting, and something may be truly wrong with the values and behaviors with which we are raising our children; but they just think it is absolutely fantastic to smash a tall tower to pieces. And I'm not gonna lie, I kind of like it too. It's fun to watch something be smashed to pieces. When super slow motion cameras first came out, I watched this video of a water balloon exploding in slow motion over and over again. It was amazing. To watch it stretch, stretch, stretch, and then . . . pop! A million droplets of water exploding in every direction slowly falling to the ground. It was so cool.

When I was in high school, I watched the Cincinnati Reds stadium being demolished. To watch what had been carefully designed and built with incredible amounts of labor destroyed in seconds was unreal. Years of memories and so much history, and then it was gone. (I just went to YouTube and watched it again. Still cool!)

When it comes to what initiates the process of deconstruction, we fall into three possible categories:

1. Those who will proactively want to pull apart their beliefs and initiate the process on their own.
2. Those who realize because of an event or circumstance that a belief doesn't fit and needs to change.
3. Those who will have someone else smash what has been built into pieces.

We don't always neatly fit within one of the groups, because there will be different reasons why we begin the deconstruction process throughout our lives. When we're in the first group is when we'll feel the healthiest. When we're in the second group, we are far better off getting through the process than burying our head in the sand, but it may be more painful than we would like. I believe that a lot more of us are in the third group than we would ever realize.

I could win an argument in the area of theology with the vast majority of people. That's not speaking to my intelligence, it's simply speaking to my education. I have spent far more time learning about theology than most people have. The key? It doesn't really matter which side of the argument I have to argue for. I can usually win. My ability to win an argument doesn't have anything to do with me being correct, it only speaks to my education.

When I leave for work in the morning, I am not dressed for battle (I'm not going to try to Jesus juke you with a riff on the full armor of God). I'm dressed in jeans, converse shoes, and a dress shirt most days. If I came across someone fully outfitted for war—dressed from head to toe in armor, outfitted with weapons, and ready for battle—I would lose! I would lose mightily! Does this mean they are a better fighter than me? Does it mean that they are right and I am wrong because I lost the battle? No, it simply means they were prepared for war, and I was prepared for work.

That's what has happened for many people within their faith. People have been taught how to live out their faith, how to own their faith, how to share their faith, but never how to defend their faith. As a result, someone who specialized in being able to attack someone else's faith won an argument (or to be more accurate, intellectually bullied them). This is not to say we should re-orient our Christian training to focus far more on apologetics; it's simply to understand the process by which many of us lost our faith.

Many of the speakers/teachers/thinkers who have contributed to the total deconstruction of someone's faith were prepared for war. They did not have passive thoughts about a life of faith, they were angry about it. It's not enough for them to not believe in a higher power, they have to smash your beliefs as well.

The assumption behind this is that when it comes to matters of faith, we'd all be better off with an empty Lego set. Nothing constructed, nothing built. Just a blank sheet. That's how the world will function best, and that's the only way for us to be truly "objective."

Instead of fighting against these modern-day intellectual bullies, I'd like to entertain their thoughts. Because I think we should. It's healthy. Christianity has absolutely impacted the world, but would the world be better if it was rid of the impact of Christianity? If we all had an empty Lego set, what would it really look like?

The World Without Christian Beliefs

I used to work out of a Barnes & Noble. A couple of days a week, I went there to write. The coffee shop area was right across from the social sciences section. When I'd get stuck writing, I'd kind of stare off into the distance and try to gather my thoughts. Almost every time, when I'd begin recollecting my thoughts, I'd realize I was staring at a book by Yuval Noah Harari titled *Sapiens*. I remember being fascinated by the subtitle, "A Brief History of Humankind." It wasn't the wording of the subtitle that caught my attention; it was that a book 580 pages in length could be described as "brief." That was all the motivation I needed to pick it up.

Throughout this book, Harari shows what the world looks like when we see it from a purely biological perspective. One of my favorite parts is when Yuval describes how the

Declaration of Independence would be re-written from a secular perspective. The Declaration currently reads, "We hold these truths to be self-evident, that all men are created equal, that they are endowed by their Creator with certain unalienable Rights, that among these are Life, Liberty, and the pursuit of Happiness." Whether you agree or not as to whether the United States is a Christian nation (which may be the most pointless debate ever), all of us should be able to see the presence of Christian values within this statement.

Harari's recommended rewriting of the Declaration is as follows: "We hold these truths to be self-evident, that all men evolved differently. That they are born with certain mutable characteristics, and among them are life and the pursuit of pleasure."

More biological? Yes. More poetic? That's up for you to decide. There are however, two massive differences that I want to discuss.

The first is that "the pursuit of happiness" is rewritten as "the pursuit of pleasure." According to a purely biological perspective, happiness is not a "thing." It's not a state, not an emotional high point, and certainly not the result of a life well lived. Biologically there is only pleasure. We can measure the amount of pleasure in our lives.

Before inserting my own experiences and perspective within this discussion, I want to ask you: Is that what you've found in your life? Are you the "happiest" when you have sought to maximize pleasure? When the pursuit of your life has been to do things you want, you desire, and you enjoy, has it automatically resulted in happiness?

Me? I am at my "happiest" through self-abandonment, not self-fulfillment. When my life is focused on serving those around me and loving them well, I have continuously been the most fulfilled, the most joyous, and as crass as it sounds, the happiest.

I did not say that I am my happiest when I am serving others, which is the conclusion that we often jump to. We think if we go volunteer somewhere, we'll feel better about ourselves. No, I am at my happiest when I am caught up in something bigger than myself and am quite clearly no longer thinking about myself. When my plan and agenda are no longer the focus of my life is when I am the most fulfilled and the least anxious. But if we strip Christianity out of our worldview, we are left only with "the pursuit of pleasure." We are left with running from experience to experience, hoping to make ourselves feel alive, fully knowing that the law of diminishing returns is working against us, and we will have to find something else in the near future to increase our pleasure.

Is that world better? Would you rather live in that world than this one? Even more importantly, would you rather live in that world than the one God is inviting you to help create?

The reality is when it comes to casting aside our beliefs, we often do it halfway. We rid ourselves of the common practices and behaviors of a Christian life, yet we maintain the values of a Christian worldview because we don't realize how tied together they are. But over time, Christian values will fall away if they don't have the Christian life to support them. What we need to wrestle with is the question of whether or not that world would be better. And if that first part on happiness bothered you, this next one really will.

In the re-written secular declaration, Harrari rewrites "all men are created equal, that they are endowed by their Creator with certain unalienable Rights" to "all men evolved differently." You may think, "Why did he rewrite the first section but not the second? Why did he change 'endowed by their Creator' to 'evolved differently' without rewriting 'all men are created equal'"? This may be the greatest assumption we make about our world—that being equal isn't tied to the life of Jesus. There is no second section without the first.

Without a belief that we have been created, there is no inherent value in each individual. The Christian teaching says God is the creator, and because God is of infinite value and because He created you, you automatically have value. Your life has value regardless of what you do with it. Your life should be viewed as sacred, and it holds the utmost significance, completely disconnected to what you do or do not accomplish. Put very simply: You matter because God created you.

I have four kids. Currently they are eight, six, four, and two. When people ask me, "Why do you have four kids?" I simply say what I know they're already thinking. "Because we make bad decisions." It's a lot more fun to answer that way. Now, we do make bad decisions, but my four children are some of my best decisions. My kids are everything that small children are supposed to be—crazy, wild, fun, hilarious, obnoxious, nerve-wracking, exhausting, and joyous. My kids are unique, as every child is, but my kids also have a special value to me, a special significance, because they are mine. I tell my kids constantly, "No matter what you do, no matter what you become, you are always welcome here." While I don't think the younger ones understand the importance of this statement, the eight-year-old has picked up on it. She's beginning to realize that she will always be accepted, always loved, that she has infinite value regardless of any of her faults, failures, anything that happens to her, or anything she does.

This is what God believes about you. At the end of creation, God looked at the man and the woman and said they were "good." We spend so much of our lives attempting to be *good*, do *good*, or act *good*. The truth is that God has already said that we are good, that we were created with value and infinite worth.

If that perspective, that worldview, is tossed aside, then so is the understanding that every individual has "certain unalienable rights." Why? Because these rights are "endowed by their creator," not by society. And instead of "all men are created equal," we are left with the idea that we "evolved differently."

I was having a conversation with a friend recently who had left faith behind. We were discussing many of the ideas that have turned into this book but specifically, the theory of evolution and the idea of the "survival of the fittest." My friend had an extremely hard time digesting my point that survival of the fittest and love your neighbor are ideologically opposed to each other.

What? Let me explain. Jesus taught that we are called to love our neighbors as ourselves. And he is not the only one who said that. The golden rule has been taught in various religions and public elementary schools for quite a long time. But the golden rule is mutually exclusive with the idea of survival of the fittest. You cannot believe in both macroevolution and the idea we should care for the least of these.

Imagine you're in a third-grade classroom. The teacher is finishing up the lesson on evolution. She's just taught the principle of survival of the fittest, which states the organisms that are best adapted to their environment will continue to exist, while those who aren't will become extinct. After this lesson, the kids line up for recess, and their behavior has been poor recently, so she reminds them about the class rule: Treat others as you would like to be treated. What?!

In the animal kingdom, the weakest, slowest, and dumbest of a species are allowed to die off. In some species, the weakest members of a pack are killed off to keep from slowing everyone else down. It is in a word, ruthless. If you are slower or dumber than everyone else, then you're not helping, and you need to go.

As my friend and I sat at Waffle House discussing this idea, he hated it. There was nothing about it that he liked. But he couldn't refute it. The best he could muster up was, "Well maybe we've evolved to the point that at the apex of evolution, we're now understanding how to take care of each other." Let me translate what that means. "Maybe at this point in the evolutionary process we can go against all the rules that have defined the evolutionary process." That obviously is not going to be the case.

At the end of the day, without the belief that worth is given from above, we are reduced to believing whoever is the strongest and smartest should leave the weakest behind. And the only argument we can give for why the world should be different is because it "should." No other principle, no other belief, and no foundation on which to base acting for the good of common humanity, other than we "should."

That should be a terrifying realization.

In the movie *Avengers: Infinity War,* the villain Thanos pursues eliminating half of the population in the universe. But he doesn't view himself as the villain; he views himself as the savior. He is not a bloodthirsty executioner. Rather, his character watched his home planet be destroyed due to overpopulation and wants to save the universe from the same fate. His end-goal is to reduce human suffering, but his means is through genocide.

Here's the question: Is he wrong? If we take a purely biological view of the world, the answer is no. No, he is not wrong. His plan would, in the long run, provide for the greatest potential for a species to exist and would, in the short-term (after the initial genocide), dramatically reduce human suffering caused by the limited carrying capacity of the Earth.

But this question just floats in the air, and our only real response is that the Avengers "should" stop Thanos. Why? Because he's wrong? Based upon what foundation?

In an article appearing on *Forbes*'s website, JV Chamary asks, "Is Thanos right about killing people in '*Avengers: Infinity War*?'" Here's his very thoughtful statement dealing with this complex ethical question: "Thanos thinks the solution is simply to wipe out half the population. This fictional scenario is *obviously wrong from a moral perspective*, which is why earth's mightiest heroes try to stop him." While I will acknowledge that the focus of the article is more about the carrying capacity of earth as it relates to overpopulation, I believe this is a thoughtless response to the ethical question.

Why is it "obviously wrong from a moral perspective?" If you have a Christian worldview then your answer is because we are "created equally and endowed by our creator with certain unalienable rights." But if there is no creator, Thanos makes sense.

We see this moral question in other movies, such as *Kingsmen*, where twice, there is a plan to rid the world of people who are causing problems and the Kingsmen sweep in and save them because they "should." We see it in political discussions about the "super-rich," and the question, "Should we work for wealth redistribution?" We say no one "should" need that much money or they "should" give the money back to society and those who need it most. The response of the top one percent, if they desire to keep their current ridiculous standard of living should be, "You believe in survival of the fittest? We are the fittest." Without a foundation of the belief in the intrinsic value of each individual, any act of charity is an act of foolishness that goes against natural selection.

While the previous examples deal in the political and philosophical realms, there is another real life example of this moral question, which is extremely disturbing.

In 2016, the Cincinnati Zoo made international news for all the reasons it did not want to. On May 28, a three-year-old boy climbed into the gorilla enclosure where a seventeen-year-old male gorilla named Harambe was kept. Not only was Harambe a key attraction at the zoo (I had taken my kids to see him several times), but the zoo staff hoped he would produce offspring. All of these hopes were dashed when the three-year-old climbed into his enclosure. After the gorilla drug the boy around for a period of time, a zoo worker, fearing for the boy's life, shot and killed the gorilla. This was an incredibly tragic event, but what amazed me was the response.

Investigators interviewed a number of primatologists and concluded that the zoo had no other choice under the circumstances. They explained that while it was a tragic event, the gorilla would have certainly killed the boy. Director Thane Maynard stated, "The child was being dragged around . . . his head was banging on concrete. This was not a gentle thing. The child was at risk." Jane Goodall said in an interview that the zoo had no other choice but to kill Harambe. Even Jack Hanna defended the zoo's action, calling it the "correct decision."

While the experts agreed that the risk was too great not to kill the gorilla, that risk was more than worth it for others. I live in the Cincinnati area, and for over a year after the event I heard people argue that the life of the gorilla was worth more than that of the boy. He was a silverback gorilla who would be able to extend his species, and there are lots of little boys.

There is a piece of this argument that makes sense. It actually makes perfect sense as an anonymous observer, but not if you're a parent. Especially, if you're that boy's parents. There is no question that the zoo made the right decision. Because regardless of how rare any species is, you know that little boy has value, infinite value.

As we've explored the ways in which our society has inherited Christian values that will not be able to stand without a quickly eroding Christian foundation my question is this, "Which world do you want to live in?" Do you want survival of the fittest or love your neighbor? Do you want a world that is ruthless or one that is kind? Because they cannot both exist.

As we deconstruct our faith down to nothing, we think we are moving to a more evolved perspective. But that's only because we don't realize how ingrained and rooted Jesus's values are in our current worldview.

In the empty Lego set, there is life and the pursuit of pleasure, but there is no hope.

CHAPTER FOUR

THE CONFESSION

I sat in the parking lot waiting for some satellite to find me. No, I'm not a spy. I'm just terrible with directions. My sense of direction grew worse once I realized my wife was aware of my failures and would just tell me where to go. That's not a complaint; she should tell me where to go. It doesn't make sense for us to drive in the wrong direction because of my foolish pride. That's just to say that any hope I had of becoming better at directions has long vanished because now, I no longer pay any attention to where I'm going because I know I'll be told where to go.

There's a scene from the American version of "The Office" that I really resonate with, especially when driving. (Most people would just say "The Office," but it feels more culturally significant to differentiate the American version from the British version.) Michael and Dwight are out on sales calls together and are discouraged by their lack of success compared to their more technologically advanced competitors. The GPS they are using tells them to turn right. Michael and Dwight disagree as to whether it means to make a direct right turn or to merge toward the right. Michael's point is that the GPS said to turn right, so maybe there's a shortcut. Dwight's point is that there is a lake directly to the right of them. Michael turns right. Dwight screams, "There's no road here!" and they drive straight into the lake.

That's how much I trust a GPS. It's a drive-into-a-lake level of trust.

So I'm sitting in the parking lot of downtown Columbus, and I have the address typed into where I need to go, but my location services cannot figure out where I am. Therefore, knowing where I need to go is moderately worthless.

I know that when I pull out of the garage, the satellites will find me (through magic) and I'll immediately have my directions. (Hang with the metaphor for just a second; we're going somewhere.) When I know where I want to go but not where I am, I could eventually figure out the way to get there. If I try enough routes and make enough turns, I would eventually get to where I wanted to go. But that process would be far longer, and far more frustrating, than it needed to be. It's always easier to get to where you want to be if you first know where you are.

So here's my question: Where are you in terms of faith? And maybe more importantly, how'd you get there?

First, "Where are you?"

Are you hopeful, optimistic? Are you longing? Are you so turned off and disenfranchised with the entire thought of a belief system that you have no interest in even having the conversation? Or perhaps most importantly, are you mad? The realization, if you're mad, is that we don't get mad about stuff that doesn't matter to us. Any time I'm mad, I'm simultaneously acknowledging that I deeply care about what has happened. So if you find yourself in a spot where you no longer have the faith you once had and you're mad, you need to know that means that you care. You may have no idea why you care, but you do.

Where are you? There's a version of this question that long-time church members used to ask each other. "How's your soul?" It's a powerful question, but we rarely ask it. Even more infrequent than the number of times we ask this question are the times we pause to honestly answer it.

How's your soul?

Relieved? Bitter? Full? Running on fumes?

J.R.R. Tolkien described how I often feel through one of the most accurate metaphors in the modern world. His hobbit, Bilbo Baggins, is at a pivot point in which he has concealed a secret from his friends and family for many years. The pressure of this secret, and everything that comes with it, has worn him out. In a moment of clarity, he answers the "How's your Soul" question. "I feel thin, stretched, like butter scraped over too much bread." We would say, "I feel worn out, exhausted, like I don't have enough to keep going."

Is that you?

It's always easier to figure out how to get to where we want to go if we first know where we are. In many ways, you can't know where you want to go until you know where you are.

This is the confession that makes all the difference.

When we think of confession, we typically think of owning up to what we've done wrong. We think of apologizing to a friend or going into a booth with a priest sitting in the other side and telling him all of the terrible things we've done. But confession is so much more than that. Confession enables progress, and confession is the one thing that must be in place in order for growth to happen.

Whenever I do counseling for married couples, one of the first things they will tell me is how committed they are to each other. It's their weird way of feeling they're bringing some measure of virtue and strength to their marriage because usually they act terribly to each other. "It may be hell at home, but hey, at least we're committed! Nothing is ever getting better, but we said we'd promise to try, so here we are." I'll explain to them that while commitment brings stability to a marriage, only confession can give it health. To be committed doesn't do you any good if where you are isn't a good place. But if confession enters into the equation, all of a sudden, we have an opportunity for things to improve.

The most important question is *where are you*, but maybe the best way to answer that is by asking, "How'd you get here?" How did you get to where you currently stand? The status of your soul . . . what made it that way?

I think it is helpful for everyone to wrestle with these two questions. Sometimes a counselor can offer a great deal of help in answering these questions. But in lieu of us having a personal counseling session, I want to offer two stories that may spark some thoughts as to where you are and how you got here.

Starry Night

For as long as I've been in ministry, I've had a picture of Vincent Van Gogh's painting, "Starry Night," hanging in my office. Sometimes, it takes people by surprise because I'm not the most culturally refined person. I don't keep it there because of my love for impressionist, or post-impressionist or whatever kind of painting Van Gogh did. And strangely, I don't keep it there because of my love for the painting, I keep it there as a reminder of how much damage a leader in the Church can inflict.

Internet articles tell me that the Church is the key piece of the painting. There are rolling hills and swirling clouds but only two vertical pieces within the painting—the tree and the church. We all notice the tree because of its massive size, but the church becomes the natural focal point for your eye because of its vertical dimension and location on the painting. The painting was designed to draw your attention to the church.

Van Gogh painted "Starry Night" in what we would consider strange circumstances. It was 1889, and Van Gogh painted it from a room in the mental asylum at Saint-Remy where he was recovering from mental illness and the self-inflicted amputation of his ear. He was isolated in his room and would stare out at the night sky then paint what he remembered during the day. If you looked at the view from his window, you would see the obvious similarities between the landscape and what he painted. But there is one key difference—the church. There is a church outside Van Gogh's old window, but it is not the church in the painting. The church in the painting is the church from Van Gogh's childhood.

Van Gogh didn't start out his adult life as a painter. He came from a long line of Dutch Reformed pastors. Van Gogh himself trained for the pastorate and was dejected when he was turned down by the Church. Instead, he chose to work and live as an evangelist among the poor. Van Gogh gave away almost every single thing he owned in an effort to aid those around him. The church authorities who had commissioned him for this work went to check on him one day, and upon seeing the conditions he was living in

pronounced him, "unfit for the dignity of the priesthood."
Van Gogh had trained to be a pastor and was rejected by the
church, then gave his life to serving those around him and
was rejected by the Church again.

While the church becomes the natural center of the
painting, you might notice something else important if you
look closely. There is no light. All of the other buildings in
the town have a light on except the church. This is the most
profound statement Van Gogh could make on his views of
faith. There is no light.

I keep that painting as a constant reminder of the damage
that Christian leaders can do. I know that for all the potential
I have to do good in the world, I have a greater potential to
do harm. The first line of the Hippocratic oath for doctors
is, "First, do no harm." The same should be true for pastors

There has been an edited retelling of Van Gogh's story
that goes like this, "He came from a long line of ministers,
but he didn't have the interest in faith they did and slowly
turned away from his faith." But that's not true. There was
an event that led to his divorce from faith. There was pain,
brutally inflicted upon him when he was doing exactly what
he should have been doing because a Christian leader did not
responsibly do what they were called to do. He left because
someone did harm to him and his faith.

Is that what happened to you?

Is there hurt in your past from religion? Did someone
you looked to for spiritual guidance cause your pain? Have

you ignored the hurt because that is easier? I think we've edited our own stories in much the same way that people have edited Van Gogh's. We tell a story of slowly drifting away from the faith because of disinterest or lack of relevancy, when the truth is there is often pain in our past that has never been dealt with. That has never been confessed.

I've been going to a recovery group for the last couple months. I'm not exactly sure what I'm in recovery from . . . the truth is lots of things with control probably being the greatest. I don't go because of an acute pain caused by an addiction; I go because I love the people there. Their honesty, their optimism, their energy—I love it. They have a saying that goes, "You're only as sick as your secrets." As soon as I confess my struggle, confess my addiction, confess my hurt and my pain, I can get better. But if I don't, I stay stuck, I stay where I am. I stay unhealthy. Commitment gives us stability, but only confession can give us growth.

I've found that many people who believe that the light is out in the church came to this conclusion through an emotional experience before they had an intellectual observation. Instead, they tell a story about coming to a logical conclusion that faith isn't true, necessary, or beneficial. And while they may have come to that logical conclusion, there is often a history of emotional disruption that paved the way for that to happen.

I hope this hasn't happened to you. I deeply hope that someone did not misuse his or her position of spiritual influence to cause damage to your faith, to cause damage to your life, and to inflict pain upon your soul. But the reality is that spiritual malpractice is alive and well, and many people have been the victim of either intentional or collateral damage from those actions and those people.

If that is your story, I am so sorry.

And my plea to you would be to talk to someone about it, work through it with a counselor, and at least confess to yourself the damage that this has done and the pain that it has caused. But please, do not ignore it. Please don't brush it off and act like it never happened or that is was really nothing. You may not want to go back and relive those memories and revisit that hurt, but there is healing there. Sometimes taking a step backward is the best way to move forward. Remember, as my recovery friends say, "We're only as sick as our secrets."

Tea Cup Overflowing

There once was a man who went to a monastery to seek a spiritual director. Upon meeting with the monk who would become his spiritual director, he confessed to him the struggles going on in his life. He told him of all the pressure he was facing in every arena of his life and the toll it was beginning to take on him. The monk sat there and listened patiently as the man continued on, and when he was finished, the monk pulled out an empty cup and poured tea into it. The man seeking direction watched as the cup filled more and more, while the monk's eyes remained on him. He grew uneasy as the tea reached the very top of the cup, and the monk still wasn't paying attention to the cup but continued looking at the man who was seeking direction. Then the tea began to overflow the cup, all over the monk's hand and arm and then dripping in puddles onto the floor. All the while, the monk stared back at the man. Finally, the man seeking direction couldn't take it any longer and shouted for the monk to stop, that the cup was full, and it couldn't take any more. It was at that point that the monk stopped pouring the tea, looked at the man and said, "So it is with you."

Within the pages of Scripture, we find a rhythm, which our lives function best in—work and rest. Six days of work, one day of rest. A day of work and a night of rest. We're better this way; we're healthier this way. But we've abandoned it. Andy Crouch says that we have replaced this work/rest rhythm for a new rhythm—toil and leisure. We're never really deeply engaging in anything and never really recovering. We live in an eternal purgatory, one in which we're never engaged but never disconnected. We encounter a non-stop barrage of texts, emails, notifications, activities, and engagements, and the tea spills out of the cup because there is no room left.

There's a beautiful story Pastor John Ortberg tells about when he called up his friend Dallas Willard. John desired the pace of Dallas's life and the pace of his ministry. He talked about attempting to cram into his life all the activities of soccer, piano, school, and expected spiritual health on top of all that. He ended this with a question. "What do I need to be spiritually healthy?" There was a long pause on the other end of the line. Then Dallas Willard answered, "You must ruthlessly eliminate hurry from your life." Ortberg said there was another long pause after that and then he said, "Okay, I've written that one down. That's a good one. Now what else is there?" After another long pause, Willard responded, "There is nothing else. You must ruthlessly eliminate hurry from your life."

This is not a point of productivity. This is not, "You accomplish more by doing less." This is a plea that your soul was not designed to always produce and to always engage.

When I allow (key word here is *allow* . . . no one can force an overfilled life upon me. I have to allow it) my life to spill out everywhere because it is too much, I find that I become numb. I don't laugh as much, I don't hurt as much. Desensitization doesn't happen because of the things we've been exposed to. Desensitization happens because of overexposure to everything. Good things, bad things, beneficial things, and painful things. All of it becomes too much, and we weren't designed for that.

This desensitization becomes deeply problematic for the development, and even the sustainability, of our faith. While I believe our brains must be fully engaged in the process, and we are to use logic in every part of our faith, at the core, faith is an act of the heart. It is the culmination of our emotions. I have found that the people who have the hardest time moving toward a place of belief are not those who have intellectual objections or those who have emotional hurts, but they are people who have no passion in their lives. It is the dulling of the senses and this dilution of our emotions that becomes the greatest hindrance for God to work. This is why, in Scripture, we frequently read this chilling phrase, "Their hearts were hardened."

If we were honest about our lives, we'd confess that our hearts have not just been hardened to faith, they've been hardened to everything. Before too long the overwhelmed life will lead you to numbness and cynicism.

Again I need to ask, "Is that you?" Do you have trouble feeling? Are you instantly skeptical about anything? Or everything? You may not say you're not instantly skeptical about everything, but if you think about it, you can't remember the last thing you *didn't* have cynicism about. You may have perfectly good reasons for why you think that way. You may have a solid logical argument for why your intellectual position of cynicism is the most intelligent one. I get it. I've been there.

But how's your soul?

The Journey Back

Reliving these moments can be difficult, uncomfortable, and painful. Going back through the moments of our lives when we have attempted to forget isn't fun, but it's important. Inspecting our lives to see if we've allowed ourselves to become overwhelmed or to see if we've allowed our schedules to become numbing agents isn't easy. Sometimes, we need help from others in the process.

It wasn't easy for me to see that I had become the cynic whom I detested. It was hard for me to admit that I had ceased to be "The man in the arena," whom Roosevelt referred to in his famed speech in France, and instead had become the one who points out "how the strong man stumbles." It isn't fun and it's not easy but it's important. If I'm unable to confess that I don't want to always be where I am, then there is no growth in my life. And where there is no growth, there is no hope. So I need to be honest; I need to confess.

Sometimes, we need people to point out what we can't see. Are we mad? Are we cynical? Are we numb? Sometimes we need others to help us work through what we can't process. But this process is important: It's much easier to get to where we want to go, if we first know where we are.

So where are you?

How's your soul?

How'd you get there?

CHAPTER FIVE

QUITTING THE WRONG THINGS

Faith should never make your life smaller. If faith shrinks your world, if faith shrinks your possibilities, if a belief in Jesus reduces your dreams, then it's not faith.

Look at the first disciples. Did their world grow smaller because of whom they were following? Of course not. One minute they were fishing day, after day, after day. The next minute they were meeting people they would have never met, going places they would have never gone, and witnessing things they couldn't have even imagined. You may contest what Jesus did because a life of endless fishing sounds pretty close to paradise for you (gross), but you have to admit that their lives were bigger as a result of meeting and following Jesus.

But that's no longer how we typically see Jesus. Instead of freeing ourselves from oppression and expanding our possibilities, we see the decision to follow Jesus as restrictive. Faith has become focused on a morality we don't care about, obligations we don't want, and rules we don't understand. Our lives have grown smaller because of our faith, not bigger. We've exchanged imagination for certainty, dreams for commands, and adventure for duty.

Just like the disciples did. Right? Obviously not.

A simple, but important thought: You're not simply called to believe in Jesus but to follow him. Yeah, we know that. But the implication is that if your life *looks* and *feels* nothing like Jesus' life, you're probably not following him.

Now, do we know *exactly* how Jesus felt? Of course not. But we do know that he experienced the full spectrum of emotions—joy, grief, love, pain, and heartache. They were all there. But that's not what many of us experience. Our boring and restrictive version of faith has left many of us not just joyless but emotionless as we trudge through our lives.

My point is not that all of faith should be easy. My point is not that the entirety of our lives should be described as "happy." My point is certainly not that there shouldn't be boundaries and restrictions when it comes to our understanding of morality.

My point is that we've quit the wrong things.

There are parts of our lives that we have eliminated in the name of faith, parts we were never meant to get rid of. Faith was meant to make our life bigger emotionally, relationally, intellectually. We weren't meant to quit the part of our lives that were true just because it didn't line up with someone else's experience. While there is a ton of a material that could be covered on this idea in this chapter, I'd like to explore one area in particular—science. Some of you have already intellectually worked through this process, but I still hope what I can add may be helpful and encouraging to your faith. For those who haven't worked through this process, or who have abandoned their faith because of the claims of science they couldn't dispute, I hope this serves as a much-needed life raft.

Science

Faith and science are not opposed to each other. If there's a possibility that a scientific discovery would destroy your faith, then you don't have the faith that Jesus desires for you.

My fundamentalist friends who take every piece of the Bible completely literally will disagree with this, and I'm okay with that. I'm okay with that for two reasons:

1. This book isn't for you, and
2. You're wrong (That felt a bit heavy, but let me explain)

Is it possible the Earth was created within six days? That the Earth is only 6,000 years old? Is it possible that through Scripture and science, we can date the exact start of the universe? Is it possible that through the prophetic words of Scripture, we can specify the exact date that Jesus will return? Maybe. And that's not just an indifferent maybe, that's a shrug your shoulder, turn your head to one side, furrow your eyebrows, and raise your voice to a high pitch kind of maybe. One that communicates not only do I not know if that is true, but I'm quite convinced it doesn't matter. That kind of a maybe.

If I had the faith of a fundamentalist, my world would have been rocked a couple decades ago when I found out that Genesis 1 is a poem. (Say what?) You heard me; it's a poem. (But it doesn't even rhyme!) I know. Genesis wasn't originally written in English (nor was Jesus an American citizen, but we'll get to that later), so when the Jewish scriptures were translated form Hebrew to English, we lost the nuance of the artistic form. But Genesis 1, in its Hebrew form, is a poem.

If you were attempting to communicate very important, very specific, scientific information, would you write a poem? You might if you're a kindergarten teacher and want your kids to remember the information. Or possibly if you're a

Southern Baptist preacher just because anytime alliteration is a possibility, you just can't help yourself. For the vast majority of the population, not so much.

Some may contest that we are supposed to read the Bible literally. We are to do exactly what the Bible tells us to do. And you are exactly right. But we really need to clarify what that means.

When I ask my kids if they're hungry, and they say they're starving, should I rush them to the emergency room to fill them with nutrients? Of course not. And it's not because my kids are exaggerating (and sometimes have a martyr complex), it's because that's not what my kids are attempting to communicate. They're simply attempting to tell me that they are, indeed, really hungry. If I say I'm as hungry as a horse, do we take that as scientific statement? Absolutely not. We understand what I'm attempting to communicate the magnitude of my hunger.

A number of years ago, my wife and I were in a social situation that I didn't want to be a part of. There were a whole bunch of people I didn't know in a room, and I don't love being in a room with a whole bunch of people I don't know (you can give me that pastor of the year award later). I thought my wife was enjoying it because she is an extreme extrovert, so I left. I found a side room and played on my phone, passing the time in a more delightful manner. It turns out, she wasn't enjoying herself, and I had actually left her in an awkward conversation that she didn't want to be a part of.

So later on, as we're recounting this story to our friends, my wife described the situation by stating, "Then Kevin literally threw me under the bus!"

My friends looked at her confused, as they should have. As should anyone if that statement was literally true (get the pun?).

I corrected her in the kindest way possible. "I did not *literally* throw my wife under the bus, I quite *figuratively* threw her under the bus." My friends were less shocked and my wife had about the same feeling of upset, so I'll call it a win!

My point is a literal understanding of Scripture must take into account the author's intent. You are not being true to what is communicated if you assume that someone is actually starving, someone is actually as hungry as a horse, or that someone was literally thrown under a bus. That's not what is being communicated, so to assume that is not only unhelpful, it's dangerous.

Genesis 1 is a poem. We might disagree on *everything* the author was communicating, but everyone should be able to agree with the fact that the author was communicating that God is the Creator. That God existed before time and that part of God's actions were the creation of the universe.

How did God create the universe? I'm not so sure. Seven days, seven time periods, Big Bang, evolution, or with a magic wand? I'm really not sure. But I'm confident He did.

One of the pastors at our church was having a conversation with a friend who had left the faith. When asked why, he responded, "I just can't disbelieve all the things that science has to say. I can no longer ignore science because I say I believe in God." This may be your position, too.

Here's the beautiful thing: You don't have to throw the facts away. You don't have to suspend your understanding of the findings in Science *because* of your belief in God. The first scientists didn't, and you don't have to either.

Alfred North Whitehead, the famed philosopher of science, said that science required Christianity's "insistence of the rationality of God." He described how two fundamental beliefs of Christianity led to the scientific process:

1. Before Christianity, there was a belief that all of history was cyclical, that we were just running in an endless hamster wheel condemned to eventually repeat the same mistakes of our ancestors. But with the arrival of Jesus this set an understanding that history is linear, not cyclical. There is progress, an evolution to mankind, and that we are heading somewhere. (It's a hilarious thought, given how many Christians perceive science today, that Christians were the first to believe that mankind was evolving). It was this understanding that the world is headed somewhere that led to the desire to continuously research, test, and improve upon what had already been done.

2. Christianity's insistence on a Creator led to the belief that if God is the Creator, it is partially through His creation that God makes himself known. So the work of a scientist was not very different from the work of a theologian because at the end of the day we're all just further discovering who God is and who He created us to be.

Powerful, right?

If science and faith were opposed to each other, then how is it possible that some of the most famous scientists throughout history were believers in Jesus Christ? Leonardo da Vinci, Nicholas Copernicus, Galileo, Isaac Newton, and George Washington Carver are just a few of the scientists throughout history who saw the work of science and theology as aligned.

I would love to go through the most recent studies in psychology, conflict management, human interaction, and leadership to see how they line up with Scripture. I would love to see how the most cutting edge discoveries just reconfirm what has always been in the pages of the Bible.

Did you know that you can't be stressed and grateful at the same time? Because of how our brains are wired, it is impossible to feel both gratitude and stress at the same moment. Scripture tells us to rejoice always and not to fear. How about that. (Notice my period. It's not a question.)

As I read through the latest findings in science, management, sexuality, and economics, I'm not afraid of what the Bible has already said because I have every confidence that it will be confirmed.

And you shouldn't be afraid either.

Faith is not restrictive; it makes life bigger. There are some who will attempt to spend their lives answering questions on the origin of the universe through the explanation of science, but they still can't come close to giving an adequate answer for why we are here or why we should get out of bed every morning and live our lives to the fullest.

Faith answers what science can't, and science answers part of what faith hasn't. There is nothing in your life that you experience that will be contradicted by the pages of scripture and who God has revealed himself to be. No emotions, experiences, memories, or discoveries will change what God has shown us is true. Now, they may help us reinterpret what we thought was true- leading us to see that it was our interpretation of life (or worldview) that was off.

Faith is bigger than what our minds can comprehend. Faith expands our lives. It expands our perspectives, and it expands our possibilities, so quit reducing it. While quitting the wrong things may be one piece of the deconstructed tower that led to your faith crumbling, my guess is this next chapter will show where it really started falling apart.

CHAPTER SIX

HOW FAITH REALLY DIES

The stories we tell ourselves matter. We use stories to make sense of the world and to give our lives context and meaning. We tell ourselves stories about our lives and about others' lives. We tell ourselves stories to make sense of where we are and to make sense of what has happened to us.

When it comes to our past, we continuously tell ourselves a story that has a common formula. "Because of _____, I am _____." Because of this bad relationship, I am more cautious and guarded with my trust. Because of this fantastic coach, I am more likely to try my hardest for an authority figure. Because someone told me I'm not good enough, I am more likely to stick with what's comfortable. Because someone told me I'm not good enough, I am more likely to want to prove everyone wrong.

We tell ourselves stories in order to find meaning and gain context, and the fantastic thing is that we get to decide the meaning these events have in our lives.

This is one of the most important lessons any of us can learn: You cannot control the events that have happened in your life, but you do get to decide what meaning those events have. You get to choose the impact those events have through the stories that you tell.

Was it all your fault? Probably not. Was it all their fault? It could be, but again, probably not. Is this a setback or a time when you were strengthened? Are you lost or searching? Those are different perspectives to the same situations. You get to choose which story you tell.

This is both beautiful and concerning. It's incredible that even in the hardest and most difficult moments, you get to shape what life means to you. It's beautiful that the scars you carry can move from reminding us of pain to representing strength. It's beautiful those moments of pain can become reminders of positive times. Difficulty can become gratitude through the stories we tell. But in the same way that it's a good thing—that we can shape the meaning of the stories we live out—it's also very concerning as to how easy it is for us to shape the details of the stories themselves.

As we assign meaning to our stories, there is a revisionist history we can easily fall into, which results in changing the story itself. Once we arrive at a meaning that we're comfortable with, we often rewrite the story to fully fit that meaning.

We see this all the time. I watch with amazement when some professional basketball players seem to believe they have never committed a foul during their entire careers. A decade in the NBA, and every time the ref blows the whistle and points at them, they are amazed, shocked! How could this be? Because the story they tell themselves always puts them on the right side.

That's a goofy example, but my guess is it's not hard for you to think of all the ways you've seen people do this. The person who always ends relationships because the other person was "crazy," the person who can't keep a job because their boss is always a narcissist, the friend who judges others but never seems to handle constructive criticism themselves, and the list could go on. What has happened is that we've taken a good thing—the ability to shape the meaning of our stories—and turned it into a dangerous direction, the ability to shape the details and facts of our lives. We no longer simply assign meaning to our stories. We begin to edit and rewrite the details of the stories themselves.

This understanding is important for life, but it is absolutely essential for understanding faith. You see, when someone falls away from faith, loses their faith, or just no longer believes, he or she tells a story. They tell themselves a story to make meaning of the events that just happened and to explain how they ended up where they are. And we are chronically misguided on the narrative about how faith dies.

Here's the story I hear the most: "I just quit believing." I heard something. I read something. I listened to a lecture. I had a long conversation with a friend who had preciously fallen away from the faith. And then . . . I didn't believe anymore.

The emphasis within these stories is always on the *moment*. Inherent within these stories is a "crisis moment" in which someone realizes he or she no longer believes. By the nature of the way in which these stories are told, this moment was inevitable. There was no going around it. I used to believe, but now the facts became indisputable, and I no longer had a choice.

My guess is that regardless of where you currently stand, when it comes to belief, you have stories like this. I do, too. Moments in which our faith was being challenged internally, moments in which we struggled to believe. Sometimes it's because of outside information we sought out, but even more often, it's because something happens to us. Someone got sick. Something bad happened. Something good you anticipated, hoped for, dreamed for, and *prayed* for didn't occur.

And then our faith was gone.

And the story that we tell is, "Because of _____, I could no longer believe." Once I heard this, or discovered that, or went through this event, then belief was simply impossible. I want to believe, I wish I could believe, but I can't now. Not after I've seen what I've seen and gone through. Not after what I've been through.

Here are the two things I want us to be aware of:

1. The meaning we create from our stories is that our faith was no longer "logically possible" because of what we've learned/experienced.
2. The detail we tell ourselves is that we *lost* our faith in the moment.

You know what's interesting? The language we use in these stories—our faith is *lost*. Not left but lost. Because we tell a story of removing faith from our lives, of deliberately casting it off because we had become more enlightened than our Christian beliefs. But when we actually get to the moment to describe what happened, we use a term that claims no responsibility. Lost.

Interesting.

There's a book I try to read about every other year titled, *Leadership and Self-Deception*. It's kind of about leadership, but it's really about self-awareness and how we cannot understand self-awareness until we understand the stories we tell ourselves. They explore this fascinating idea: the more I act against the way I think I should, the more I find reasons to justify what I'm doing.

The greedier I am, the more I see the world as greedy and can justify my greediness. The more selfishly I act, the more I see everyone as selfish and acknowledge my actions as the natural outcome of the way the world is, not the way I am.

What they speak about is a fascinating idea. It means our thinking doesn't drive our actions nearly as much as our actions drive our thinking. I love listening to sports fans argue. It's amazing how much they can disagree about the officiating within games. And why is that? Is it because they understand the rules differently? Of course not. It is because they are so emotionally invested in their teams, that it changes how they view things. Richard Rohr says it like this: "We do not think ourselves into new ways of living, we live ourselves into new ways of thinking.

When Jesus invited people into relationship with him, his language was simple. "Follow Me." To the fisherman he said, "Follow me." When speaking metaphorically, he said, "My sheep hear my voice, and I know them, and they follow me." With slightly different terminology, he tells the disciples that he is not just the truth and the life but also "the way."

The initial invitation of Jesus is not to believe in him in a logical, factual manner but to be invited into relationship with him—to walk with him, see where he goes, and live life like he does. For the first disciples, this looked like physically following Jesus around. For all the disciples since the 1st

Century, this has been about living out the teachings and life of Jesus as we "keep in step with the spirit." (Gal 5:25)

But whether you are doing this in the 1st Century, the 21st Century, or anywhere in-between or after, the invitation is the same—into relationship with Jesus. To follow him.

Here's my guess. (I could be wrong, but I've seen this story play out over and over again.) Long before you quit believing in Jesus, you quit following him. Long before you came to the intellectual conclusion that Jesus wasn't real, you gave up on a relationship with him.

People tell themselves the story that their faith "was lost" in an inevitable crisis moment when they came to the intellectual decision that Jesus isn't really the Son of God or didn't rise from the dead or that God isn't real. However, these same stories are significantly predated by one more of the following things:

- A lack of participation in the local church.
- A loss of diligence in personal spiritual practices.
- An addiction that turned their focus and pursuit of joy away from Jesus (often alcohol or pornography).
- A relationship (often romantic) that consumes all of their time and attention so that they begin to base their self-worth and emotional stability on that other relationship.
- A general drift from the life that is defined by a relationship with Jesus.

You get to decide the meaning the events in your life have, but you don't get to change all the details and facts to support the meaning that you want to fit. That is nothing other than self-deception. And that's what the real story of deconversion is often about. We want to do something else with our lives, so we quit.

We don't quit believing, we quit the relationship. And eventually, we think we no longer believe.

Faith is never less than an intellectual pursuit, but it is always more. You don't have to throw out logic to believe, but you do need more than logic. Because Jesus didn't invite you into an intellectual exercise; he invited you into a relationship.

So let's be honest. Is this your story? Not the one you've been telling yourself, but is this your *real* story? Did you try to poke holes in your belief to excuse your actions? Did you dive deep into a super liberal theology that is the equivalent of no belief system whatsoever so that you could paint everything as gray and do whatever you wanted, only to wake up one day in a crisis moment, realizing you actually believed in nothing?

I often talk to pastors who think that people need to be *convinced* back into faith. That's a faulty assumption because most people were never convinced *out of faith*. We quit the relationship, and then we quit believing, in that order.

We didn't leave our faith behind, and we didn't throw it out. We lost it.

We describe it the same way a couple that was married describes their divorce. They *fell* out of love. They didn't decide that the other person was no longer worthy of their love, but they lived in such a way that didn't value the other person, and over time, they quit loving them. The process was then revealed in a single moment. "I no longer love them, I'm not happy, I want a divorce." We get divorced in a moment, but it wasn't inevitable. We quit the relationship long before we say those words of finality.

We don't quit loving in the same way that we don't all of a sudden quit believing. We fall out of love, and we lose our faith. Because we quit the relationship.

But I have good news for you if you're willing to read further.

You might have given up on God, but He hasn't given up on you (and never will).

CHAPTER SEVEN

DOUBT

Doubt is healthy. Doubt is natural. Doubt is the context for faith. If there is no doubt in our lives, then we're not being honest about our faith and our faith cannot grow. We need doubt.

But we should not be obsessed with doubt.

We should not spend all of our time focusing on the questions that we cannot answer. We should not spend a bulk of our mental space on the answers that do not make sense. We should acknowledge doubt, confess our doubt, and converse about our doubts, but we should not become pre-occupied with our doubts.

There is a false narrative that has been going on for a while now. I don't know exactly for how long it's been going on, but I know my parents lived it, I've lived it, and the generation after me is currently living it out.

The narrative goes like this: When I was brought up in the faith, I was taught what I believed and what I didn't believe. I accepted these doctrines on faith, like any kid accepts information from his or her parents. In the same way that I learned sixty minutes make an hour, even though I had no idea what a minute was or why it was that length of time, I accepted that Jesus was part of the Trinity and that there were three persons to the Trinity (Father, Son, and Holy Spirit), and they are all God. But I don't know if I believe that now, and honestly, I don't even think I know what that means. I've talked to a couple of my friends, and *they* don't know what it means *either!* We've realized that we have doubts! And we're going to express them. Even though generations before us were never okay with acknowledging any of their doubts, we're not going to be those people. We're going to be the ones who are willing to share our doubts.

This would be accurate, if ours was the only generation to tell this story. But we're not. Everyone seems to think they're breaking the mold of all those who went before them by being willing to express their doubts. But we're not.

C.S. Lewis struggled with doubt. Mother Teresa struggled with doubt. Abraham and Sarah struggled with doubt. Moses had doubt. You're not the first, and you're not the last because doubt is healthy.

Other books will cover how to wrestle with your doubt and how to express your doubt in a healthy way. For the purpose of this book, I want to focus on what the false narrative of "we're the first person to ever express our doubt" has done to our faith. Back to Lego sets.

When you're building a Lego set and realize a piece is in the wrong place, you have to begin un-building to get the piece in the correct place. As previously stated, this is deconstruction—when something previously unquestioned is now questioned, and we begin pulling apart what had previously been put together. Whether this process comes from (1) a significant experience that makes us reconsider what we once were so sure was undeniable true, (2) when our perspective has been broadened and we have to hold together the possibility that two seemingly mutually exclusive ideas can now fit together, or (3) when we grow up and we have to replace our childhood beliefs with adult ideas, the feeling is the same—doubt.

When we believe the narrative that we are the first person to express our doubts, then our tendency isn't simply to deconstruct that part of our faith but to deconstruct all of our faith. We think that because we are the first people to ask these serious questions, then we have a moral obligation to question absolutely everything. So we pull everything apart back to the point where nothing can be trusted, all truth is relative, and no one can really know anything.

But you don't have to do that . . . nor should you do that.

The apostle Paul had doubts. That's right, the man who came to faith through a radical encounter with God on the way to murder and imprison Christians had doubts. His doubt gets expressed in two ways, past doubts that are now answered and current things he still doesn't understand.

Past doubts that are now answered: Sixteen different times throughout Paul's writings in the Bible, he refers to a "mystery." In his letter to the Church in Ephesus, Paul refers to this mystery seven different times. He refers to the mystery as Christ himself, what Christ is doing, and what Christ has done. Then he tries to be as clear as he can in verse 6, Chapter 3 of Ephesians with, "The mystery is that through the gospel the Gentiles are heirs together with Israel, members together of one body, and sharers together in the promise of Christ Jesus." This doesn't mean a lot to us, but it should. For generations, the Israelites, God's chosen people, had wondered how God would use them to redeem the entire world. God himself had said that "all nations on earth will be blessed" through them, but we never really knew how. It was a doubt, a cause for concern. But Paul says right here that the doubt has been removed because through the sacrifice of Jesus, God has brought everyone into the fold, everyone who believes into the promise. There was doubt, there was mystery, and now there isn't. It's been revealed.

Current things he doesn't understand: We all have the list. The list of things we don't really understand about God.

- What is the Trinity?
- How does God heal?
- Does God still heal?
- Why didn't God heal this person?
- How does God know everyone?
- Does God know the future?

We have our lists. I don't understand why, when Jesus went to the pool of Bethsaida, he only healed one person. It says there were "crowds of sick people," but Jesus only heals one. I don't understand. Paul never gave us his list. I'm pretty confident he had one. But he never hands it to us.

Instead, he says, "For now we see in a mirror dimly, but then face to face. Now I know in part; then I shall know fully, even as I have been fully known." Paul makes this utterly brilliant confession. "God knows me better than I know him." He trusts that in this moment, God knows him in his entirety, that he is "fully known," Yet, he acknowledges that he doesn't fully understand God. He sees partially, he understands incompletely, like "in a mirror dimly." And even within all that confusion, he trusts. He trusts that one day, he will "know fully." He trusts that what he currently grasps only part of, he will one day completely understand. But right now, in this moment, "God knows me better than I know him." And that's okay.

It would be helpful if we could all take the Apostle Paul's posture when it comes to doubt. Some of Paul's doubts are diminished, but not all of them. Some of them are gone, but some doubt remains, and just because some doubt remains doesn't mean he had to throw everything else out and start all over. Paul acknowledges that when it comes to faith, we don't have to know everything in order to know something. We don't have to know all truth to acknowledge that something is true.

Every question you have doesn't need to set off an existential crisis about the meaning of life. While God promises that some things can and will be known, we will not understand everything. Like Job, we need to acknowledge that we won't always understand "the deep the things of God" because we're not God! We dimly see in a mirror. We do not yet understand fully. And that's okay.

Let me press this further.

The modern deconverted Christian has now taken the same posture as the people whom they held the most contempt for—the fundamentalist Christians. Allow me to explain.

For a fundamentalist to believe, every piece of his belief must fit perfectly together. This makes a fundamentalist unusually prone to catastrophic damage to his faith when it comes to the process of deconstruction, which we will all go through. As soon as one belief is removed, the whole thing immediately comes crashing down. It's as if their faith is built with the same construction as an arch. If even one brick of an arch is removed, everything will crumble. There is no room for uncertainty, no room for mystery, and no room for questioning.

Many deconverted Christians have taken the same posture. People within this group often claim to love "mystery," but rebel against anything that can't be properly explained. The deconverted claim is to search for a deeper meaning, and yet these individuals insist there is no meaning if they cannot adequately understand it. The deconverted Christian often speaks of wanting a mystical faith, yet rejects every doctrine that even hints at something supernatural.

This leads us to the arrival of those who are "spiritual, but not religious." They are spiritual in the sense that they'll send me thoughts and good vibes, but they don't really believe that there is a divine force that intercedes on our behalf. They are spiritual in the sense that they will search for the transcendent yet reject everything that doesn't have a rational explanation. Spiritual in the sense that they will find the spirit at work in a concert or in a community of people in which they sit with an assigned seat and had to buy a ticket for but reject all forms of worship that are organized by a local church because those are programmatic and emotionally manipulating.

Job asks, "Can you find out the deep things of God? Can you find out the limits of the almighty?"

God answers, "Who is this that questions my wisdom with such ignorant words? You are God's critic, but do you have the answers? Brace yourself like a man, because I have some questions for you, and you must answer them."

Of all the statements God makes in Job 38–41, there is one proclamation I find most disturbing.

You are God's critic.

I've spent much of my life as a cynic. I've claimed to believe while silently judging. I've prayed for God to be close, to be near, to give comfort, and to give peace because I didn't really believe that He still moves and heals, and I could explain away all of those other prayers. I've sat in the back of worship experiences and judged everything and everyone in the room. I chalked the work of production teams up to manipulation and labeled the response of those around me as naive. There were parts of my faith that I believed, and there were parts of my faith that I doubted. The parts I believed were the parts I could understand. And everything I couldn't understand, I learned to throw away.

I was God's critic. I thought I could do His work better than He.

Let's remember, the great sin is not disbelief. The great sin is not a failure of faith. The great sin is pride. Pride is what kept me from knowing God and trusting Him more than anything else. Pride is not content with simply knowing the

Creator of the universe; it must also understand everything. As C.S. Lewis wrote, "As long as you are proud, you cannot know God. A proud man is always looking down on things and people; and, of course, as long as you are looking down, you cannot see something that is above you."

For my entire life, I have been fascinated with stories of faith. I've heard countless stories of conversions, and countless stories of deconversions. But in all the stories of deconversion, not a single person has mentioned pride. No one has ever said that the obstacle to their faith was their own personal arrogance. Note this—for two centuries, the leading Christian thinkers (from Augustine to Lewis and others) have identified pride as the utmost sin, one that will keep someone from knowing God. But I have heard of no one, not one single person, who was able to identify the role that pride played within his or her loss of faith.

We disguise pride as doubt, failing to see the clear distinction between the two. Doubt is the result of a healthy intellectual pursuit when things don't make sense. Pride is the belief that we are entitled to know and understand everything. We don't throw our faith away because of doubt; we can live in the tension of ideas that don't make sense. We throw our faith away because of pride.

I hear constant conversations about the messiness of faith, about how it's not supposed to be neat and tidy, not all supposed to fit together, but it's supposed to be messy. Like Jesus. Jesus was willing to deal with messy people and messy situations, and we'll even say "get messy himself." "He who knew no sin but became sin so that we could become the righteousness of God." That's messy.

Doubt is willing to wade into the messy. It's the will to embrace the messiness of faith. Pride cannot do this.

Before we jump to the next chapter, to the next section, I want to ask you some questions and leave you with one idea. This would be a good time to pause. I never put a book down when the author tells me to put the book down. I think, "I know better! Forget them!" And I keep reading. I'm still pretty cynical. What you do is up to you. But I'd encourage you not to move forward until you actually know which side you fall on.

Do you have true doubt, or is it really pride masquerading as doubt? Are you a self-proclaimed mystic who denies all supernatural components of faith because you really are more of a fundamentalist than someone who is spiritual? (Yeah, I said it). Are you willing to allow your beliefs to be messy?

I'm tired of spiritual people who deny the supernatural.

I'm tired of cynics reducing the conversation down to only what can be logically observed.

I'm tired of Ego putting on a nametag called "doubt" and acting like it's smarter than everyone else.

I know God. I have a relationship with Him. I don't understand Him. I know parts of His personality and His character. I know what He has revealed through His Word, through my experiences, and throughout history. And like the mark of any great learning, the more answers I receive, the more questions I gather. This is true of my relationship with God. I know Him, but it's messy. And that's okay.

You don't have to understand everything in order to believe in something.

CHAPTER EIGHT

BUILD AGAIN

started drawing a couple years ago, and I'm terrible. I'm okay with being terrible. I used to draw when I was younger. Everywhere I went, I brought a pad of paper and a pencil with me. Restaurants, church, or friends' houses. I loved it because I thought drawing was fun. Then I remembered seeing drawings from some other people, people who were better than me. So I quit. I had this idea in my head that if I couldn't be the best at it, there was no point in doing it—that it was a waste of time.

No one directly told me this lie, but many people fueled that idea over time, albeit inadvertently. I'd go to a museum on a field trip and people would talk about how incredibly difficult it was to get a picture in a museum. What I heard them saying was, "This is incredibly important so value it." I learned and believed, "Only a few people actually get to be artists, and you're probably not going to be one of them." I had this idea that the purpose of creating art was to be able to make a living off of it (every professional artist just rolled their eyes, I know). So I quit.

Years later, my daughter started to draw. She wasn't just coloring pictures or doodling on a blank piece of paper, but she really took an interest in it. I watched her sketchpad go with her to different places. I noticed piles of pictures scattered across the house. She'd spend most of her time at home watching YouTube videos about how to draw different characters.

So I did something I hadn't done in two decades; I started to draw with her. I plopped down right next to her on the couch, grabbed a piece of paper, a #2 pencil, a book to write on, and attempted to draw ponies with my eight-year-old. And you know what? It was fun. I liked it. I still wasn't good, but I no longer cared if I was good. I was no longer doing it to build a career but rather, to simply allow myself to enjoy it.

My purpose had changed, and as a result, my outcomes changed. What I gained from it is different.

This is true in all of life. If you change your purpose, you'll change your outcome. No, the tangible result may not be different. No one has paid me for a drawing (YET!). But what I experience and what I personally gain from the process will be different. If I go into a new job expecting to be deeply satisfied, then I will always be frustrated. But if I go into that same job seeking to be helpful, I will be satisfied. New purpose, new outcome. If I go into a relationship seeking to have all my needs met, then I will always long for a better relationship. But if I go into a relationship seeking to love, I will find fulfillment. If I seek what I can gain, I'll never have enough; if I seek to give, then I'll be joyful with what I have. New purpose, new outcome.

But what do drawing and purpose and outcomes have to do with faith?

Everything. (Seriously, everything.)

Most people enter into faith seeking answers, answers to big, existential questions, such as, "Why am I here? Why are we here? What is my purpose?" Answers to practical questions, such as, "Which job should I take? Should I move forward in this relationship?" Answers to philosophical questions, such as, "Why do bad things happen? Why did God allow sin to enter the world?" And answers to pressing questions, such as, "Why did they get sick? Why did the accident happen? Why did they die so young?"

Seeking an answer to one of these questions is usually the reason why we go *back* to church or open up the Bible for the first time in years or schedule an appointment with a religious leader. If the outcomes we experience are shaped by our purpose, it's important to acknowledge that for most of us, our purpose in faith has been to find an answer.

And sometimes we find it, sometimes we don't.

Hear me out. I grew up in Sunday School. I'm aware that the answer you're supposed to give to every question is Jesus. Who made the world? Jesus. Who offers forgiveness? Jesus. What has a bushy tail and collects nuts? Sounds like a squirrel, but hey we're in church, so Jesus. (I know, that was lame.) But this is what people who grew up in church are taught: Jesus is the answer to every question you have. While that statement sounds like it is full of faith, it's actually misguided and inaccurate.

The distinction that must be made is that when people say, "Jesus is the answer to every question" (which they shouldn't), they don't mean that Jesus is the explanation but that Jesus is the one we should turn to. Our response of "Jesus" is not an answer but points us in the direction of the one whom we should trust.

Still stuck on Jesus as the answer? Try these on for size:

- Which job should I take? Jesus
- Why do bad things happen? Jesus

- Why did the accident happen? Jesus
- Why did they die? Jesus

Isn't that some beautiful theology right there?

If our purpose in approaching faith is to find accurate answers to the questions we're asking, we're going to become frustrated at best and far more likely we'll end up leaving the faith entirely. If that is our purpose, that will be our outcome. And if you want your outcome to change, you have to change your purpose.

What if the purpose of faith isn't to give us better answers but to give us better questions? What if the outcome we are after isn't a desire to be "right" or "sure," but what if the outcome is a life that is bigger than the one we previously held onto? What if the true outcome of the Christian faith lived out properly is a life bigger than we ever could have imagined?

Most of us walk through our lives in pursuit of the answer to this very elusive question, "How can I be happy?" We look for work that is enjoyable and fulfilling, we look for relationships that are fun and easy, and we attempt to construct our lives so that we feel happy as we go through our days. Most of us fail.

We're not happy, we're not fulfilled, and we're not enjoying the lives that we live. Kind of amazing to think that the one question most of us are pursuing is the one question we are failing to answer. As Americans, we literally wrote it into the Declaration of Independence. We believe we have the right to pursue happiness. We have the right to pursue it, but the problem is we're just not that good at finding it.

When the central question you're seeking to answer is "How can I be happy," you're left with a pretty small life. Every relationship becomes a pursuit of how can this person make your life better. Every opportunity is met with "will I find this enjoyable?" What do you do when your marriage is no longer making you happy? The answer seems to be that you should abandon it and find a new one. What do you do when your job is no longer bringing you happiness? Quit and apply for a different one. You may eventually come to the understanding that personal growth and service bring happiness. But when everything you do and become is ultimately focused on your enjoyment, you are living a very small life.

Think of the questions we ask:

- "What will make me happy?"
- "What will help me advance?"
- "What will get me noticed?"
- "What will make me famous?"
- "What will entertain me?"

These are the most common questions humanity asks itself, and they're all so small!

Even their more evolved forms aren't that much more impressive:

- "What will help me grow?"
- "Where do I belong?"
- "Where can I make a difference?"

If you've grown to the point that you're now asking the latter set of questions, your life will feel bigger than before. But it is still a small life. So where do we go? What do we need to ask?

There's this pivotal moment within the accounts of Jesus' life. Jesus has just performed several miracles in the region of Galilee and is headed to Caesarea Phillipi. As he and the disciples are walking along, he stops and asks them a question. This is important; this is rare. Jesus asked many questions throughout the gospels, but they were most often in response to a question that was posed to him. To get a better grasp on how significant this is, Jesus asks 307 questions throughout the gospels. He is only asked 183 questions. Of those 183 questions, he only answers three. When Jesus asks 307 questions but only answers three, that should make us reconsider whether the purpose of faith is about having the right answer or asking the right question.

But you already know where I stand on that issue.

So Jesus and his disciples are walking into the region of Caesarea Phillipi. I'm sure they're a little tired but still a little thrilled at all they've just experienced. Jesus initiates a question. He asks, "Who do people say I am?" In other words, what's the word on the street, what do people think about me? They answered with the common thoughts of that day, "Some say John the Baptist, some say Elijah, and others say you are one of the other prophets." Scattered thoughts but a clear answer: He is one of the resurrected prophets of old who has come back to them. A position of influence and certainly of power but still . . . just a man.

So he asks them the most important question, "But who do you say I am?" He's really saying, "You've seen the miracles. You've heard the teachings. Most importantly, you know me. Not just my power and my knowledge but you know me personally. You haven't just heard about me like a lot of people, you know who I am." So he turns the question from asking them about the rumors on the streets to a personal question, "Who do you say I am?"

If he's another prophet who performs signs, then they're really just paparazzi. They're people following him around hoping to see the next spectacle. If he's an ordinary man and all this is made up, then they're wasting their lives. If the question they are asking is, "How can I be happy?" then as soon as things get difficult they will fall away. Forever. As soon as following Jesus no longer brings recognition, they'll leave because it's no longer enjoyable. If he's just a man, then it's really obvious when it's time for them to exit. As soon as it's not fun anymore. Because if Jesus is just a man, that's about as big as our lives get. Eat, drink, and be merry for tomorrow, we die.

Jesus turns the question, the most important question, personal. He asks, "Who do you say I am?" Peter clears his throat. Everyone looks at him as he collects his thoughts. He knows how he's going to answer, because I'm sure he's thought about it for a long time now. But it's different to voice it. It's different to say it out loud. He musters the courage and speaks as clearly as he can.

"You are the Messiah, the son of the living God."

The implications are astronomical. Peter is saying, "You're not just a man. I know you're here in flesh and blood but somehow you're more. You're the one who was chosen, the one who was sent. You're God himself here on earth, on two legs and two feet. You're heaven here in our midst."

And in that moment, his life got bigger. A lot bigger. Not prosperity gospel bigger. Not God's blessing will be through financial gain bigger. That's still a small life. His life was way bigger than that.

Jesus replied, "You are blessed, Simon son of John, because my Father in heaven has revealed this to you." He did not learn this from any human being.

And here's where it gets really good . . .

"Now I say to you that you are Peter (which means 'rock'), and upon this rock, I will build my church, and all the powers of hell will not conquer it. And I will give you the keys of the Kingdom of Heaven. Whatever you forbid on earth will be forbidden in heaven, and whatever you permit on earth will be permitted in heaven."

Jesus, in one statement:

- Changes Peter's identity through his name.
- Declares that Peter is foundational in the building of the church.
- Gives him authority to shape the direction of the church.

All because he answered a *better* question, "Who do you say I am?"

I mean, come on! That's amazing!

So when I ask you, "Are you happy?" it seems like a pretty silly question at this point in time doesn't it? When you realize that our actions have eternal repercussions, it seems foolish to make decisions that are simply in pursuit of our current enjoyment.

Many people view a life of faith as a restricted life. Too many do's and don'ts and too many rules. "I could do so much more if I wasn't giving away ten percent of my money." It's viewed as too small a life. But somewhere within what we read as restrictions, we have missed the point. I'm not giving away ten percent of my money, I'm giving away my life! It's not about trying to live on ninety percent of my income and be morally upright. It's about a complete and total emptying of myself in order to be used by God for His purpose.

I can't remember the last time I asked myself if I was happy. I am, though. I am really, really happy. But that's not the point. It doesn't even matter. There are bigger, more important, questions to pursue.

- "Is my life true?"
- "Does my life matter?"

And these questions begin with this one from Jesus: "Who do you say I am?"

When we quit building a life of faith, we reduce the scope and significance of our lives. When the Legos have been torn away, and there is nothing left but the base, we have two options about how to view it:

1. It's so much work to rebuild, and we're just at the start, or
2. It's completely empty and anything can happen.

This is my plea to you: Begin building again because your life is bigger than your pursuit of happiness. Because you were meant for more. Because the questions that we are asking from our lives are not worth living for. Because our lives were meant to be bigger. That's what faith does.

Three days ago, a man whom I had never met walked into my office. He'd been coming to our church for the previous eighteen months, but we had never met. He told me his story. He cried, I cried, and all over again I was blown away at the way in which God works.

He said he'd been coming to church to appease his wife. His wife wanted their family, particularly their kids in church, so he went to make her happy. He never believed. He couldn't believe. He harbored too many doubts. Too many questions on the integrity of Scripture and on who Jesus is. There were too many things that didn't quite make sense.

Then a couple things happened that made him ask important questions. He was out late one night drinking with some friends, and when he arrived at home, his wife asked if he'd been out with another woman. He was mad. "I mean, I don't even have time for that." (I thought that response was hilarious.) He said after a couple hours sitting in his anger, his wife's question began to bother him. He asked himself, "What kind of man have I become that my wife would have to be concerned about that?" I wish more people had the perspective to ask that question. It's a good one. The day after that great question, his son came up and asked if he wanted to go outside and play catch. The man told me he made an excuse, saying he was too tired. As his son walked away, he thought, "What kind of a man have I become that I make an excuse to get out of playing catch with my son?"

The following day, he was sitting in an empty parking lot. Alone. Thinking about his life. Thinking about what he had become. He told me his dad had passed away twelve years earlier. He had been close to his dad, so he did something he hadn't done in the past twelve years. He spoke to his dad. Out loud. He asked him, "What on Earth should I do?" That's when he started crying. An audible answer came back, clear as day, in his Father's voice.

"Believe."

That's when I started crying.

We wiped our tears. I gave him a hug, and then we laughed.

He told me he had no idea what to do now. He had no idea how to pray. So I set him up with some people who could walk with him, had him start reading the scriptures, and explained what he should focus on in the days ahead. As he was leaving, he said something I will always remember.

"I can't wait to see what God is going to do in my life."

A bigger life.

A man who went from trying to pass the time and attempting to make excuses to get out of his responsibilities, which should be his delight, finds faith and "can't wait to see what God is going to do."

I don't want you to begin rebuilding your faith because Jesus is real. He is, but that's not the "why." I don't want you to begin rebuilding your faith because Jesus is true. Again, he is. But that's not the "why" either.

I want you to know the unbelievable joy associated with a life that is fully conscious of the eternal implications of the days we are living in. I want you to know the deep meaning that only comes with a life that is aware of the purpose for which God has created you. I want you to wake up believing that your days matter. I want your relationships to be filled with passion and purpose. I want your actions to have energy behind them. I want you to be able to do more than find a life that is simply enjoyable.

Your life is bigger than that. Jesus created you for more than that.

It's time to build again.

CHAPTER NINE

THE PROBLEM WITH TOWERS

I was sitting in the sanctuary of our church, talking with a man whom I had just met. In the six minutes we had known each other, we had laughed, cried, and embraced. That's quicker than my slightly introverted self likes to progress in a relationship, but it was fitting. You see, this was his first Sunday *back* to church. His story was a little different from most. He did not drift away from faith; his faith came crashing down. His deconstruction wasn't like a Lego set, it was more like Jenga. One piece had been removed, and the whole tower came tumbling down. And the piece that brought it all down? The Trinity.

Here's how I teach people about the Trinity: "God exists as three connected, but distinct, persons. They are all God, but they are not the same as each other. There are God the Father, God the Son, and God the Holy Spirit." Then I tell people, "Think of an apple. An apple has three distinct parts—the skin, the flesh, and the core. The core is not the flesh, and the flesh is not the skin. Each part does a unique thing and can be distinguished from the others, yet they are all an apple. That's the basis of the Trinity, but to be honest, I really don't understand it all."

(And everyone just questioned why you have read this far!)

Let me explain. I believe God has revealed Himself to us. I believe God desires to be known by us. I believe the greatest revelation He has given to us is through the second person of the Trinity, Jesus the Messiah. But just because God has allowed Himself to be known, just because He desires to be known, it doesn't mean that He will be fully understood. There are parts of God's character that are beyond our comprehension. For me, the Trinity is one of them. I don't understand it. I believe it. I see evidence of it throughout Scripture, but I still don't fully grasp it. I am one person. I exist as one person. I don't really understand how one being can exist as three persons. I don't "get" it. And I'm okay with not "getting" it.

When I first started the conversation in the sanctuary, it was all about what this man was experiencing now. The grace he felt he had left behind was now so fresh to him. He experienced the sense of community, felt by gathering with the people of faith to lift our voices in praise. His description lay primarily in the arena of his emotions. But eventually, we made our way back, back to what caused him to leave in the first place—back to the Trinity. My new friend, who had just come back to church for the first time in years, wasn't okay with not "getting" it. His faith was not merely intensely logical, it was only logical. It wasn't emotional, nor was it relational. God was a concept, an idea to be studied. A theorem to be understood. And when he realized that there was an essential part of who God is that he couldn't understand . . . Jenga. When your faith is only logical, you cannot hang on to faith when there are pieces that you don't understand. For him, all the pieces had to fit together perfectly; otherwise, none of it could be true.

This was the moment I realized how incredibly important the metaphors we use to make sense of our lives are. Rob Bell taught us this (I hear the sarcastic gasp. Whatever your thoughts on Rob Bell, just hang with me for a second because this could help.) In his book, *Velvet Elvis*. He introduces a new metaphor for understanding doctrine—springs. Instead of a tower that we build against others in order to keep people out, he asks, what if we thought of doctrine as springs? Springs like on a trampoline. Springs that allow us to go higher and higher and see from new perspectives as we are elevated. It's an interesting way of thinking. Instead of seeing how we could attack someone else's faith, it would posture us to see what we might learn.

You see, as my friend described his deconversion, he described a fortress, a tower. All the pieces had fit together, allowing the tower to reach higher and higher. The work of the Holy Spirit, the virgin birth, the creation of the world . . . each of these is an individual block in the tower. The problem with the tower metaphor is the same tower that is built up can also come crashing down if one piece is out of place. The ultimate failure of a logic-only, fundamentalist-leaning faith is that faith doesn't always fit together perfectly. It's messy.

Sometimes I do pre-marital counseling. I don't often do pre-marital counseling because I'm not very good at it, and I can only assume that I'm causing damage to these future relationships, but sometimes they insist, and I say yes because I still have enough of my self-worth tied to having people like me (how about that for confession!). When we go through pre-marital counseling, we will always, *always* uncover areas of disagreement. Disagreements on where to live, how to raise kids, how many kids, what their relationship with their families will be like, how to spend time, and how to spend money. There will always be disagreements. So I sit them down, and we begin negotiating. "She wants four kids, but he wants one; what if you settle on two kids, but he promises to give you a 2:1 ratio of holidays with your family?"

Of course I don't do that! That would be ridiculous! (Side note: Some relationships work like that and you need to go see a real counselor.) No person in the history of *healthy relationships* has ever thought, "I need to get every piece of our thinking to fit together perfectly before we move forward in this relationship." That will never happen. That's our relationships are sealed with covenants not contracts. That's why we commit before we have every detail worked out. The commitment to the other person without knowing all the details is what makes a relationship healthy. It's not just love; it's faith.

The problem with thinking of faith as a tower is that it naturally leads us into contract thinking. It leads us to a space in which we assume we have to have all the details worked out and understood in order to move forward. We've missed the most central truth of all of faith. Namely, Jesus invites you into a relationship. Not a contract, theorem, or concept, a relationship. In relationships, not everything is understood. I don't fully understand my wife, so why on Earth would I think that I would fully understand the Creator of the universe. He is beyond me, yet He invited me to know Him. Not to fully understand Him, but to be in a relationship with Him.

I love apologetics. Apologetics geek me out. I became fascinated back in middle school with the study of the defense of our faith, and I became arrogant. You see, the majority of apologetics is not written from a posture of gaining a deeper understanding of your faith but how to win an argument with someone who thinks differently than you. And there is nothing that is more misaligned with the humility that Jesus required than the thought, "Now that I know this, I'm smarter than everyone!" I made a fundamental error. I believed that growing in knowledge of doctrine was the same as growing in faith. I believed the more information I added to my understanding, the more like Christ I was becoming. I thought knowledge = discipleship. I had bought into the flawed metaphor of the tower. I was adding bricks but regressing in my faith and in my character.

The denomination in which I'm a part has us report statistics. Some people hate it, and some people think it's ridiculous. I think they're short sighted. I think numbers help tell a story, numbers help diagnose health. I've found the people who hate the stats the most are usually those who have their ego most caught up in the size of their ministries. (That was a little bit of a tangent, so let me get back to the point). One of the numbers we are asked to report is the number of people in a "discipleship environment." This is typically defined as a class, an elective, or a small group of some sort. A discipleship environment is a place in which people *learn* information together. I agree that discipleship happens in community, but I could not disagree more with the idea that discipleship is about knowledge acquisition.

When you define a discipleship environment as primarily a classroom, you have entered the epitome of tower thinking, and you are setting people up for, you guessed it, Jenga.

Dietrich Bonhoeffer wrote in his essential work, *The Cost of Discipleship,* "When Christ calls a man, he bids him come and die." To lay down self, to put aside ego, and to take up the cross. This has become essential to my understanding of the spectrum of discipleship. Discipleship is moving from "come and see" to "go and die." We move from intrigue about who this Jesus is and what this church community is all about, to personal sacrifice and a giving up of preferences and comforts for the sake of the Gospel. The initial attraction to Jesus was found in the miracles he performed. People wanted to see what on Earth was going on. But the relationship didn't stay there. It moved to later stages of discipleship marked by a willingness to be persecuted for their faith because in Jesus, they found the one who was life—and life to the fullest.

Bonhoeffer shows us that discipleship is not about information acquisition, and discipleship is not about building a taller tower with our doctrines. It's about sacrifice. It's about surrender. It's about emptying the self and being filled with Christ. It's being filled with Christ to such an extent that you would keep on rejoicing to the degree that you share the sufferings of Christ. And it's really difficult to make the focus of your faith a releasing of your ego, preferences, and comfort when you think you're supposed to be building a higher tower. It's really hard to learn surrender when discipleship has been restricted to a classroom.

If you still think you're trying to build a tower, you need a new metaphor. You need a new way of thinking about your faith.

When I do pre-marital counseling with couples, I always talk about the three behaviors that they must have if they want a healthy relationship.

1. Pray Together.
2. Bank Together.
3. Sleep Together.

They should pray together because praying out loud with and for each other is a way of intertwining our lives together in spiritual matters. I've found there are few things more powerful than praying out loud with and for the person whom you are mad at or who is mad at you. I tell them to bank together. Matthew 6:21 tells us, "Where your treasure is, there your heart will be also." We are amazingly adept at inverting the concept of this teaching. We think it says, "What you care about is where you will spend your money." It doesn't say that! It says, "Where you spend your money determines what you care about." Our wallets are not simply compasses for the direction of our hearts, they're the guides. They don't simply tell our hearts where they're headed; they can lead our affections in that direction. When couples have separate checking accounts, it creates an incredible risk for them to begin living their lives in separate directions, but one shared account changes that. People say, "But it's just easier for us to have separate accounts." It is. They're right. It is easier to head in separate directions if the relationship becomes strained and avoid all the difficult conversations that are part of two becoming one. It is much easier for two to stay two than for two to become one. Then I tell them to sleep together, but I don't think I need to get into that here.

Hopefully that was helpful relationally, but I tell you all that for a different reason than prompting the eventual conversation some of you need to have about a joint checking account. I want to switch the metaphor for these couples. I want them to get out of contract thinking because that metaphor will ruin a relationship. I want them to think of their relationship as two interwoven ropes. I want them to see that their goal is not to come to an agreement on every idea, but to see how interwoven they can make their lives. As Ecclesiastes 4:12 says, "Though one may be overpowered, two can defend themselves. A cord of three strands is not quickly broken." That's their goal, their metaphor—a life as interwoven as possible. The metaphor we use matters.

John the Baptist, when asked how he felt about losing followers to Jesus, responded, "He must become greater, I must become less." (John 3:30) John the Baptist saw that his goal was not build his platform, but to elevate Jesus. Dietrich Bonhoeffer wrote, "When Christ calls a man he bids him come and die." Bonhoeffer saw that faith was about a personal surrender and a willingness to sacrifice. The Apostle Paul, when reflecting on the actions and perspective of Jesus, said that Christ "emptied himself."

"I must become less," "Come and Die," "Emptied Himself."

It's hard to have a covenant when you keep thinking like a contract. And it's impossible to empty yourself to be filled with Christ when you keep trying to build a tower. It's impossible to become less when you're focused on what you're acquiring. And I assure you, you are not able to come and die when you're just trying to win an argument.

The metaphors we use matter. I don't think any one metaphor properly explores the depth of faith, but it's time to put the tower to bed.

CHAPTER TEN

ANCHORS

You may have heard the account of the Millennium Tower before, but the implications of it are so massive that it bears repeating. Completed in 2008, the Millennium Tower has top-notch amenities, boasts a panoramic view of the San Francisco skyline, and features multi-million dollar condos. Within the first five weeks of sales, the Millennium Tower had sold $100 million worth of condos with units selling in the range of $1.6 million to $10 million. When built, it was the fourth largest tower in San Francisco . . . but it's sinking.

Most critics say the reason for the sinking is because they never hit bedrock for the foundation. The building is anchored eighty feet deep, which is impressive. But the eighty feet means the building's foundation was packed sand. To actually get to bedrock, the foundation would have needed to be dug 200 feet deep.

While city inspectors state the building is *still* safe to live in, it has already sunk seventeen inches and tilts fourteen inches. It is currently sinking at a rate of two inches per year. Residents say they can roll a marble across their floor against the tilt and watch it move forward, come to halt, and then roll back to them, certainly a fun game to play at parties, but a terrifying game when you're 600 feet in the air.

Architects are currently proposing different solutions to prevent the sinking, but they have to rebuild the foundation. A proposed solution of drilling hundreds of steel and concrete pillars into the bedrock to stabilize the tower would cost somewhere between $200 and $500 million. Which is sizable in and of itself but especially when you know the entire skyscraper cost $350 million to build originally.

The problem with the Millennium Tower is a problem of foundation. It's not strong enough. To revisit the metaphor that we need to leave behind, this is the essential problem with towers. When there is an issue with the foundation, it is extremely difficult to rebuild the foundation, and you are not able to get back to the foundation without completely destroying the tower.

This is where constant deconstruction leads us when we believe we are building a tower—the conclusion that the foundation is faulty and the tower is unstable. So we leave it behind. Which is again, why the tower metaphor needs to go.

I know, I know. The rebuttal is "But *Jesus* used the metaphor of the tower." True, he did. He told a parable of a man who built his house on the sand versus a man who built his house upon the rock. We sing, "On Christ the *solid rock* I stand." While the importance of foundation is ingrained in our terminology of faith, and it absolutely is a common metaphor, even present within Scripture, it is not the only metaphor in Scripture. Remember, the metaphors we use are not dogmatic, they are meant to be helpful. So let's turn to what I believe is a more helpful metaphor in this case—anchors.

In the book of Hebrews, we find the writer of this letter explaining the certainty of God's promise through the life of Abraham. The writer is describing the difficulty Abraham would have had trusting God. He didn't know this God; he knew nothing about this God, and now he was supposed to leave everything he knew to follow this God who was making a promise that he didn't know if he could trust. So God makes an oath, a covenant, a one-sided promise of what He will carry out and do on Abraham's behalf. And Abraham believes.

In Hebrews 6:19, the writer gives a metaphor for why Abraham believed God. It is written, "We have this hope as an *anchor* for the soul, firm and secure." When the writer of Hebrews describes the confidence Abraham had in God, he does not use the metaphor of a foundation. He talks about an anchor. Anchors hold us where we need to be. Anchors keep us from drifting. Anchors prevent us from being tossed aside by wind and waves.

You can build upon a foundation, but when you have to tear the pieces apart because they don't fit, it will always *feel* like going backward. When we have to return to the foundation, it *feels* like we're starting over. But an anchor is something that will steady us. The link to an anchor can be short or extremely long, but either way it is always something we can return to. Anchors tether us to something solid, sturdy. A ship unanchored is at great risk of crashing in the storms, but one that is anchored can withstand the waves.

Your faith needs anchors. You need beliefs, certainties, and even experiences in which you can have full confidence. You will constantly deconstruct and reconstruct your faith. This is healthy; this is good. But if you think you're tearing down a tower, you'll be unnecessarily demotivated to build again. Switch the mental model, change your thinking, and find some anchors that you'll be able to come back to that will help you withstand the storms.

We are absolutely called to question our faith. Doubt is the context for faith. But here's the key: not *everything* needs to be constantly questioned. Doubt is healthy, but at certain points in our growth, not *everything* should be doubted. Some things should still be studied, but others should be relied upon. Some beliefs should be questioned, but others should become settled. I have now known my wife for eighteen years. Five years of dating and thirteen years of marriage, (Confession: I had to do some subtraction to figure that out, but don't tell my wife.) There are things, even after eighteen years, I don't know about her, and there are also other things that I have full confidence in. Because our relationship has been tested, and our commitment has been tried, there are things that I don't have to doubt or question anymore. That is what happens when trust is built in the relationship.

The word we use in marriage is faithful. And somewhere along in our faith, it became common to constantly call into question the faithfulness of God. We think we are like Job, who questions, but we have become more like his wife, who looks at the circumstances and says, "Curse God and die." (Job 2:9) We think we are like Job who is able to proclaim in the midst of tragedy, "Naked I came from the womb and naked I will return, may the name of the Lord be praised" (Job 1:21), but we are more like his friends whom God says, "You did not speak the truth about me." (Job 42:7)

There are parts of my faith that I question, there are areas in which I doubt, and there are circumstances in which I struggle; yet, I trust that God is faithful. I know He is constant and will do what He has promised to do. Do I believe this because I have everything worked out? No! Because I fully understand God? Absolutely not. To claim so would be ridiculous and contrary to Scripture itself. I can trust because there are parts of my faith that have been decided upon. They are settled; they no longer need questioning because they have been inspected and are trustworthy.

They serve as anchors, anchors that will keep me from drifting where I don't need to go. Anchors that will get me steadily through the storms. Anchors I can always come back to.

Your faith needs anchors.

Your anchors will be unique to you. They will be areas of your belief, your life, and your experiences where you are given an extra confidence in God. Paul describes faith as a gift. Gifts aren't earned; they are received and acknowledged. I believe you already have anchors in your life, which you can identify. They are anchors that can steady you as you are deconstructing the tower of your faith. You need to know them. You need to name them. They will get you through the times of doubt.

I have two anchors to which I can consistently come back to.

Anchor #1: Creation

I don't know if Genesis 1 is a literal account of the creation of the world. I've heard or read almost every argument as to why it is and why it isn't. My conclusion is that I really don't know. And yet within the account of Genesis 1, I have found an anchor. It says, "In the beginning God . . ."

I think the Big Bang Theory and macroevolution are fascinating. This idea that a swirling ball of mass, exploded and created all the life forms that have ever existed is really cool . . . and requires a fantastic imagination. But I've always had this question for people who use the evidence of macroevolution as the ultimate trump card to play against people of faith, "Where did the swirling ball of mass come from?" The response, "Well it just was always there?" Always there! It's the most significant scientific argument for where the world came from, the one that attempts to explain every detail and that would dismiss the notion of God, and the best response for where the ball of mass came from is, "Well, it was just there."

We have this un-debatable truth that there is something instead of nothing. And I think that's really significant. I don't get stuck on how creation was created. I'm still in awe of the fact that there is a creation! This has been an anchor for me, something I can always come back to. When the questions are overwhelming, I return to this truth: There is something instead of nothing because "in the beginning, God." And then I can go forward from there.

Anchor #2: An Experience

God has never spoken to me in an audible voice. To be honest, I really don't want Him to. Every account I see of God speaking directly to someone results in him or her being terrified. I just don't need that in my life. I have felt His presence. I have felt nudges to do something. I have had thoughts that I couldn't shake that I never would have come up with on my own. But an audible voice? Nope.

But there is an experience in my family that sticks out. I was home after church on a Wednesday night and my mom came in, sat down, and she looked to me like she'd seen a ghost. I could tell she'd been crying, but I didn't know what to ask, so I just looked at her (I've still go that going for me). To understand what I'm about to describe, you need to know that my family is very unemotional. We don't cry a ton. We laugh a lot, but there are not nearly as many tears. We're very logical. We don't do things that don't make sense, even if we want to. We're highly suspicious of people who say, "God told me to do this." There was once a lady in my church who came up to me and said, "God told me that you are supposed to mentor me." I responded, "Well, God is going to have to tell me that is supposed to happen." Harsh? Maybe a little. I just don't like people who play the God card when they want to get their way. I don't think God does either.

Now that I've given you a glimpse of the ecosystem of the house I grew up in, back to my mom. After a couple minutes of silence, she began to tell me the details of what happened. As she was driving home, she found herself caught up in her worries about a situation that was going on in our family. The details aren't important, simply the fact that this situation had been increasing in intensity and tension for the past six months and revolved around my parent's concern for the future of one of my sisters. My mom had certainly prayed about it but had also spent considerable time worrying and obsessing about it. She found herself in that same mental state of worrying and obsessing while driving home that night. I'll always remember what she told me.

"I'm driving home, caught up in my thoughts, when all of a sudden, I heard a voice say, 'Don't you hear it?' It was so clear that I immediately turned around because I was convinced someone was in the back seat (as she's driving 55 MPH). I turned back to the road and settled my emotions and then heard the message of the song on the radio. The message I had completely tuned out because of my worry, now came across perfectly clear in this moment, 'God is in control' I pulled over to the side of the road and cried because I know it's true, but somehow I had forgotten."

I've heard countless stories from people over the years of their encounters with God. Some make my jaw drop and take my breath away, and some make me really skeptical as to whether what they say could be true. But I don't need every encounter with God that someone tells me to be true. I don't doubt the presence of God because I think someone may be making it all up for attention. My mom's story may be too weird for you. It may be too cheesy. Or you may just not believe my mom's story.

But I do. I saw her face, I saw her tears, and I have no doubt that God spoke to her that night. In the midst of her worry, God got her attention and reminded her, in a powerful way, that He is still in control. And that's something that I go back to, something that steadies me when it feels like the world is caving in and my faith is crumbling. I remember that when my mom needed God, He was there in a way that she would have never expected. And it gives me confidence, it grows my faith, and it reminds me that even though I don't understand everything about Him, God is faithful.

Your Anchors

You need to find your own anchors. Or you need to clarify the anchors you already have that you may have pushed aside because you also have questions. It's okay; they can co-exist. Your anchors may be beliefs you are sure are trustworthy. Beliefs or convictions God has given you an extraordinary amount of confidence in, such as the gift of faith. Your anchor may be an experience, a moment when God spoke to you and clarified something for you. Or a moment in which you felt something or inherently knew something. Throughout Scripture, God continuously calls people to look at His past faithfulness to build confidence in Him for the present struggles. He doesn't remove the obstacles; He shows us He has been faithful and will be again, if we will just remember. We need to remember.

This isn't apologetics. Too often we attempt to build our faith by learning how to defend our faith. Faith is not an argument. It is a relationship. If your faith is built on the defense of the faith instead of a relationship with Jesus, eventually there will be an argument that will tear down the tower. If I focused more time on trying to prove my wife loved me than just developing a relationship with her, it would throw our relationship into chaos. That is not how relationships work. Jesus invited you into a relationship, not to prove a theorem. More ammunition to prove that you're right will not give you the confidence you need in the struggle.

So quit building a tower. Find your anchors. Please question your faith. But at a certain point in your spiritual maturity, you shouldn't need to constantly question everything. God is faithful, and He can be trusted. I know why I believe that, and you need to know why as well.

CHAPTER ELEVEN

A SEATBELT

W e've torn down what we had previously built up. We've looked at why. We've established anchors for our faith or have hopefully begun to look for anchors for our faith. Now how do we begin to build our faith in a way that reduces the likelihood that we'll have to tear it all down again? How do we build in a better way? How do we make sure what we're establishing isn't destined to crumble? It becomes a matter of understanding the difference between truth, opinion, and perspective; how all three of them apply to how we build our faith.

It never ceases to amaze me the way in which two people can go through the exact same situation and have two completely different perspectives. It's not just fans from rival teams having completely different responses to the call of a referee. It's the husband and wife who tell the story of the fight they had, and you're having trouble understanding how they were in the *same* fight because their stories are so different. Is the dress black and blue or white and gold? Yanni or Laurel? We are, by our very nature, subjective.

So how do subjective people approach objective truth? Some have taken the thought that believes there is no objective truth. Because we each have a unique perspective, which is skewed, there is no such thing as objective truth. But we know that isn't true. For some, this may be a contentious issue that I appear to be glossing over, but it actually isn't complicated. I may perceive the dress to be white and gold, when it is really black and blue. It can't be both; it isn't neither. It is one or the other and there is a truth behind it, regardless of my subjective perspective. Just because I have a different perspective on something that is true, does not make the truth itself subjective.

One of the most popular ideas of our age has been the notion that we have the ability to personalize truth. We'll make statements like "my truth" and tell people you need to "speak your truth." We believe in the idea that there can be such a thing as *objective* truth that only applies to us *personally*. But by definition, the phrase "my truth" is impossible. For something to be considered truth, it must be true for everyone, despite the subjectivity, bias, or opinion of some. If there is sound disagreement, it cannot be truth. It has to be an opinion. The Urban Dictionary describes "my truth" as a *pretentious substitute for non-negotiable personal opinion.* When we say "my truth," we are saying, *here is my subjective perspective, which goes against the norm that I no longer am willing to argue about because there is no chance of me changing my view, even if it's incorrect.* I know that sounds a little harsh, but if you look at the definition of what truth is, that is the conclusion you would arrive at. (If you dislike my conclusion, you probably disagree with the definition of truth, and you would like to develop your own definition, which is about as subjective as you can possibly get. Congratulations!)

There are:

- Truths: Objective claims that are correct for everyone despite any individual's subjectivity, bias, or opinion. *2+2 is always 4. Even if you say it's 5, it's still 4.*

- Opinions: Personal thoughts on how we judge something where we can clearly see why we disagree. *The Reds are the best team baseball. No they're not, you're a moron. No, you're a moron!* (That escalated quickly.)

- Perspectives: Experiences we can easily deem as true but are actually subjective. *The water is cold. No it isn't, it feels great.* The statement that the water is cold will feel like truth to you, while it is, in fact, only opinion.

The crucial point here is that we know when we're living in the land of opinions. We know when we are disagreeing over an issue and that there could be multiple defensible opinions. But we don't know when we're giving our perspective because it *feels* like truth to us. Every day, all over television, the talking heads get on and shout their opinions at each other over different issues, *convinced* they are correct, but we can typically discern when they are giving their opinions. But we don't always know when someone reports the news if they are giving their perspective in addition to the truth. Perspective is opinion that presents itself as truth. It is subjective, but it is presented and held as objective. Someone may say, "this is my truth," which means, "This is my perspective."

Once we understand the distinction between truth, opinion, and perspective, we can grasp something important as it pertains to Jesus. Scripture presents us with objective truth. Jesus himself says, "I am the way, the truth, and the life." (John 14:5) There are truths within Scripture, which are objective claims that are correct for everyone, but not every interpretation of those claims is correct. There's a common phrase that captures the idea behind this. "The Bible is the infallible Word of God, but not every interpretation of the Bible is infallible." When we read Scripture, we are reading objective truth. But here's the problem: We aren't objective; we're subjective. We have opinions about some things that we know might be wrong and perspectives about other things we are convinced are right, even though they might not be.

This leads us to the greatest problem when it comes to faith. How do I understand what is objective when I am subjective? Fundamentalists will say, "Well, just do what the Bible says."

To which I say, "You moron." (Okay, I don't say that.) "I can't always trust my perspective because I don't always know my opinion, and sometimes, my perspective masquerades as the truth." How do I know that what I believe is true? How do I know that what I believe isn't just my opinion, which I have decreed to be truth? How do I know that my interpretations, through the lens of my unique experiences, hasn't unintentionally skewed what I think is true?

Let me give you an example. A number of years ago, a well-known Internet preacher gave a sermon series titled, "Savage Jesus." The debate around this series was rousing (*sarcasm*). People on the Internet commented over and over again, "Jesus wasn't savage. He is kind and loving; he is anything but savage." Every week, the preacher would respond to the critics with a new account from Scripture, "He made a whip and whipped people; he called a woman a dog; he is not as weak-willed and soft as you make him out to be. He's savage." As you can tell, the debate was pretty helpful in gaining a more accurate picture of who Jesus was.

(Do I need to let you know this is sarcasm, or is it hopefully obvious by now.)

So how do we determine what is true? Jesus obviously believed in the utmost importance of truth; otherwise, he would have never made the claim, "I am the truth." But discerning what is true and what is perspective is difficult.

For centuries, Christianity has relied upon the Creeds to tell us what Christians have believed to be objectively true. The Apostles Creed is relatively easy to memorize because it is brief and to the point:

> "I believe in God the Father Almighty, Maker of heaven and earth: and in Jesus Christ His only Son our Lord, who was conceived by the Holy Ghost, born of the Virgin Mary, suffered under Pontius Pilate, was crucified, dead, and buried; He descended into Hell; the third day He rose again from the dead, He ascended into heaven, and sitteth on the right hand of God the Father Almighty; from thence he shall come to judge the quick and the dead. I believe in the Holy Ghost; the holy catholic Church; the communion of saints; the forgiveness of sins; the resurrection of the body, and the life everlasting. Amen."

The Creed has functionally served as guardrails for the Christian faith. In the same way that guardrails keep us from having a terrible accident by driving off the road, the creeds have kept people within Orthodox Christianity and from straying outside what Christians have collectively found to be true. They've been helpful, important, and in desperate need of updating.

(Just kidding. Gotcha!)

The creeds don't need updating, but the creeds themselves do not give us adequate resources to discern truth. They provide guardrails for belief, but we need a seatbelt as well.

While seatbelts are commonly used today as preventative safety devices to keep people from sustaining injuries, that is not the reason they originally gained acceptance. For years, drivers resisted not just wearing seatbelts, but buying cars with seatbelts. The first car that included seatbelts, not merely as an additional option but as a standard feature, was largely met with contempt. Adoption of wearing seat belts didn't come originally from everyday drivers, or even from the car manufacturers, but from racecar drivers. Sixty years before seatbelts were standard in every day cars, racecar drivers wore their seatbelts. Why? It was easier to drive at high speeds when there was a lap belt holding you in place. Seat belts weren't a safety device; they were a competitive advantage. At about the same time, fighter pilots adopted lap belts to more easily perform upside-down maneuvers.

The creeds serve as the guardrails that keep Christians from driving off the road, outside of the faith. But we also need seatbelts—ways to help us understand our belief. Things that will help us divide what is objective and what is perspective. Things, which enable us to answer complex questions without earning theology degrees (which doesn't typically help because too often people use that to make simple things unnecessarily complex).

We need seatbelts.

For years, we've used this question as one such seatbelt: "Do you believe in Jesus?" While poorly worded, what we're attempting to ask is, "Do you trust in Jesus?" Without completely revisiting our previously chapters, there is more evidence that Jesus existed than any of the Roman emperors. So we don't really know what we're asking when we ask, "Do you believe in Jesus?" That he existed? That he's Lord? It's vague, unhelpful, complex, and doesn't provide any real guidance for how we should build our faith. There's a better question, one that sounds similar but is exactly what we need.

The question isn't, "What do you believe" or even "Do you believe in Jesus?"

The question we need to ask is, "Do you believe what Jesus believed?"

When Jesus states, "I am the truth," he is telling us there is objective truth, and it is found in him. He is the source of what is eternal, unchanging, and unaffected by someone's subjectivity, bias, or opinion. It's still true. We, however, are not objective. We are subjective because of our biased perspectives. So if we are going to figure out what is objective, we don't need to focus on building a case for our own beliefs; but rather, we need to inspect Jesus' beliefs.

Was Jesus "savage?" We can go back and forth in the debate, or we can look at what Jesus said. One definition of savage is to "not be under human control." In Matthew 28, Jesus says, "All authority in heaven and on earth has been given to me." I'd say that's a yes. But another definition of savage is "a brutal person." Jesus himself says he is "the good shepherd . . . who lays down his life for the sheep." So is Jesus savage? In some definitions, yes; and in others, absolutely not! The point is this: your opinion is not what is important here.

For thousands of issues, we have wasted time and energy attempting to discover, clarify, and argue what we believe. Whether it is doctrine, beliefs, issues of justice, or issues of politics, we spend our time building the cases for what we believe. A growing faith understands that it's not about building an argument but growing a relationship. And to grow a relationship, we need to know what is true. The couple that constantly argues based upon their *perspectives* won't last long. We need truth. To grow our faith based upon truth, we need to know what Jesus believed and accept those beliefs as our own.

Now obviously, Jesus didn't speak to every issue. He didn't tell us what we should believe about every topic and discussion. But he did clarify enough to give us a foundation to stand upon. He did clarify enough that we could at least know what is objective and what is subjective. He becomes the seatbelt that allows us to go faster. He becomes the filter for separating what is an issue of opinion and what is an issue of truth.

There is a host of issues that have remained untouched—issues of substances, politics, laws, justice, sexuality, language, mercy, and economics, which I haven't touched. I do that for two reasons:

1. The goal of this material is not to address all of the hot topic issues in our culture today, but to give you a better framework for why faith falls apart, why it needs to be rebuilt, and how to rebuild it; and
2. The study of these issues is one of the primary ways that faith grows.

No, I don't anticipate you'll find a hidden Bible verse no one has seen before, one where Jesus spoke of the distinctions between capitalism and socialism and which economy is most biblical. But in the process of your search, you'll learn a little more about who Jesus is and what he wants for you. This is the beauty of this question: When we study Jesus' belief, instead of arrogantly attempting to figure out and defend our own, we are pulled deeper into a relationship with him. No matter the question, you'll learn more about who Jesus is and the character he desires for you.

God wants us to be better at relationships than arguments. He wants our faith to be stronger than our well-rehearsed defense of our opinions. He wants us to be united on what matters most and able to get along on lesser issues in which we'll disagree. For that to happen, we need to ask better questions. We need to remove "What do you believe?" as the primary question when it comes to truth and replace it with the better question, "What does Jesus believe?" And we absolutely need to ban "my truth" from our vocabulary because there is no such thing as subjective objectivity.

Get a seatbelt.

CHAPTER TWELVE
PRACTICES

This is the last chapter together for most of us. What follows this is a note for leaders in the Church, a clear call of what our leadership role needs to be in light of our own work of deconstruction. For leaders in the Church, I believe the following chapter is essential. For everyone else, you may find it helpful, but you are more than welcome to skip it.

My hope is that I've been able to identify for you the framework of deconstruction—how it's helpful, how it's harmful, and some key things you need to be aware of in the process. My hope is that you are able to grow your faith.

Maybe you were in a spot in which you had left faith behind in a messy break-up. I hope this work has enabled you to see why you made that decision and set before you a path back to a relationship with Jesus, if that is what you desire. Maybe you were in a spot in which the questions had superseded the answers, and you could feel your faith crumbling beneath you. My hope is that this work has helped rebuild the foundation underneath your feet so you can honestly ask and answer questions about your faith. I don't know where you are, but my greatest hope is that I've been able to encourage your faith in a way that it is able to move it forward.

Within that desire, there is one more important issue we must discuss—the practices of our faith. The framework we've established for how we think will accomplish nothing if we don't live in a way that is conducive to growing our faith and strengthening our relationship with Jesus. As we covered in Chapter 5, for most of us, we quit our relationship with Jesus before we quit believing in God. Our belief follows our practices. As Richard Rohr says, "We don't think ourselves into new ways of living, we live ourselves into new ways of thinking." So if we are going to continue growing our faith, we don't just need new ways of thinking, we need new ways of living.

Now, let's take a weird turn. Let's talk about mindfulness. Let's talk about the way in which we pay attention to the things we do and the way we think about what we do. Because if you simply engage in practices without mindfulness, you're going to end up right back where you started.

I realized the importance of this too late in life. It was last year, and I'm coaching my girls' 6/7-year-old soccer team. (To be clear, I was the assistant coach. I didn't want all that power to go to my head.) We're going through dribbling drills. It was a simple drill in which they practiced turning directions with the ball, a full 180 degrees, dribbling through one cone, and taking a shot at the goal. We've done this drill before. We've actually done this drill almost every week. And they weren't getting any better. The head coach (the man with the power) would throw the ball out there, and the girls would casually run to the ball, kick it backward—way further than they should—backtrack to the cone, casually dribble around the cone, and then take a shot right at the middle of the goal. We'd done this drill about every week, and every week it had about the same results.

The problem was the girls didn't know why what they were doing mattered or how it applied to a real game. They knew how to run the drill, but they didn't realize the ways in which the drill would impact their ability to score. So we did two things:

1. We explained it to them. We talked through scenarios within a game when it could be used. We asked them about times in which they were in this same situation, and they could call up times from past games.

2. We replaced the cones with people. We told the people not to move because that would be too complicated. Instead of having to picture what it would look like to move around a defender, we simply put a person right there.

Guess what happened? They got better! Quickly! They improved more in one night than they had all the other weeks combined. Why? Because they were aware of what they were doing and why it mattered. They were no longer careless; they were mindful.

I bring this up because I believe we have lost the skill of mindfulness when it comes to our spiritual practices. We have lost the awareness for which we are engaging in them. But my point in bringing this up is not to say that we need to be more aware of the practices we engage in. Absolutely not! If you walk away from this chapter thinking you need to be more intentional and less casual about reading Scripture, then you will have completely missed the direction we need to head. Again, this is not about being more attentive as we read Scripture, being more focused within our prayers, or even being more engaged within our praise. I've heard people say "don't just read the bible, *really read it!*" What does that even mean? If this is what we mean by mindfulness it'll jolt our energy for a minute that will wane as soon as the shock has worn off. This understanding of mindfulness will only have the impact of a smack in the face or cold water dumped upon you.

And my guess is, you've run this path before. You've attempted to increase your spiritual maturity through a sheer force of will. You may have even understood that your spiritual practices do not give you favor with God, that grace can't be earned. You didn't do it as a matter of salvation but you truly wanted to grow. So you engaged. You willed yourself to try hard. When things became cold, you attempted to bring a newfound sense of energy. And it waned. Because it always will.

No, our discussion on mindfulness within our spiritual practices and the way we live our lives is not about *really* reading the Bible or *really* praying or whatever other practice you want to fill in. Our understanding of mindfulness must go back to the nature of the purpose of spiritual practices themselves.

Common Ground

It's always interesting to me which sermons resonate with people and which ones don't. It's rarely the ones I would pick ahead of time. One example in particular sticks out to me. It wasn't much of a sermon; it was just a really long confession.

If I could sum-up the entire sermon in one sentence it would be, "I'm sick of me, I'm sick of us, let's cut it out." Profound, I know.

As ridiculous as that sounds, it came from a really honest and frustrated place. As I looked through the accounts of people within Scripture, I found their courage, faith, and compassion, are noticeably absent from our lives today. I read the story of Ruth, and later that day, I was counseling a man who was ready to leave his family because he wasn't getting much out of it. I had Ruth's powerful and profound words, "Your people will be my people," (Ruth 1:16) still fresh on my mind as I heard him say, "I'm just not getting much out of my family." I felt disgusted.

I noticed that in all the situations I was dealing with, an underlying selfishness was driving all of our actions and decisions. I believed wholeheartedly in Dietrich Bonhoeffer's assessment that discipleship is "from come and see, to go and die." I was just seeing a whole lot more of the "come and see" than "go and die."

I saw this not just in our lives, not just in our families, but within our faith, as well. I sat with older members of our Church who complained about the things that were changing, most significantly, the music they didn't prefer (A note of clarification: These voices are few and far between at the church where I get to serve.) Then I would hear other pastors adopt a very strict liturgical order for their service because of the rationale, "The younger generation doesn't want fog and lights, they want liturgy." I would be fine if they did it because they believed that it was more honoring to God, but their reasoning pointed to just another form of consumerism. *Church for my desires, church for my preferences, church the way I want it.*

(Heads up. I'm about to really step all over some toes right now.)

This is what I believe. I believe that churches should make every decision based upon a mission focus. I'm not talking about a carefully planned, well-crafted, beautifully displayed mission statement. I'm speaking of the common mission to which we have been called as voiced by Jesus right before he ascended to heaven. "Go, and make disciples of all nations." (Matthew 28:19)

How do we make disciples? Well, it's really, really complicated. And really, really simple. We connect people to Jesus. He disciples them, and we help. We don't disciple them to ourselves, but we disciple them to Jesus. We don't connect people to ourselves, but we connect people to Jesus. We help them move from "come and see" to "go and die."

What I say, what I felt, and what I still feel is that we're getting the "come and see" part down really well. But we're not moving beyond that.

You may hear this as an attack against the seeker-sensitive churches. It's not. It's far bigger than that. It's an all-out assault against consumerism in every form it comes in as it pertains to Church and faith as a whole.

I believe I can worship with every style of music, I can learn from every style of preacher, and I can grow through every ministry model. I can worship God with drums, organs, choirs, hand bells, or just vocals. So how do I pick which style of worship I participate in? It's simple. I can worship in any way so I choose what is most beneficial for the one who is still outside the faith. I can learn from every type of preaching/ teaching as long as it is gospel-focused and doesn't neglect the full counsel of God. So how do I pick which style of church I should go to and for me, personally, which style I should preach with? I choose what is most beneficial for the person who is still outside the faith. This is not a complicated issue.

Here's why: Church was not, is not, about me. It's not about my preferences; it's not about my desires. It's about God, and what He's doing. And the second I begin making decisions about my involvement from a perspective that is focused on my wants, my preferences, or my interests, I have made it about me. I am still coming to see, not going to die.

I believe consumer-oriented churches come in all shapes, sizes, and styles. Some of the most consumer-focused churches I have seen are filled with fog lights and a rock band. And some of them are filled with young adults who sing the hymns of old, practice the liturgy, and take communion weekly. Because not only does mission die when we focus on our preferences, but our own personal discipleship does as well. We cannot "Go and die" when we're focused on what's best for us, what feeds us, or what is meaningful to us.

The message that resonated with people was simply this: "I am tired of a faith that is more about preferences than mission, more about styles than gospel, more about placating Christians in whatever preference that looks like than taking up our cross and abandoning our personal desires to follow the path that God has called us to. I'm sick of me, I'm sick of us, so let's cut it out."

People approached me over and over again and affirmed their feelings and how they matched my own. The most common response I heard after that message was, "I'm sick of me, too." One person, who was in his late seventies, said, "If I'm going to grow, I must focus more on how my faith helps others than what I'm getting out of it." That sounds a lot like "Go and die." Another person in her young twenties told me, "My friends and I have found it very easy to bounce around from church to church, pointing out the problems in each of them and why we can't stay because it doesn't fit what we'd like. But I want a faith that is bigger than me, and the only way that's going to happen is if it's not about me. So church can't be about me either." It was fascinating. Five decades between them, and they made the same point—if my faith is going to grow, I must abandon myself.

Spiritual Practices

This brings us back to spiritual practices. A spiritual practice is an activity or exercise practiced for the purpose of spiritual growth. The most common spiritual practices are prayer, Scripture reading, worship, giving, meditation, fasting, and serving, but the list of what can be a spiritual practice is truly endless.

The purposes of the spiritual practices are to open the door to God's work in our life, to create a new habit or new routine, and to create space for a fresh practice that would allow us to be open to God's presence and work within our lives. If the spiritual practices have a mantra, it's "more of God, less of me."

One of my practices is to consistently think through what God desires to embody my life. I'm not great at meditation, but this prayer has become a form of meditation for myself. I focus on my breathing, and as I exhale, I think consciously of something that I need to be rid of if Christ is going to be fully present in my life. As I inhale, I consciously focus on what Christ seeks to fill me with. I stay in this rhythm for a long time. Exhale, inhale . . . what I must rid of, what I want to be filled with. Exhale, inhale . . . what has all too often consumed my life, the better life Jesus is leading me into.

Less anger, more peace.

Exhale. Inhale.

Release cynicism, fill with hope.

Exhale. Inhale.

Less Bitterness, more love.

Exhale. Inhale.

Earned approval, matchless grace. Judgment, mercy. My strength, His power. Comfort, growth. Activity, community.

Weak emotions, heartfelt praise. Worry, His will. Exhale, Inhale.

Less of me, more of God. Less of me, more of God. Less of me, more of God.

This is what I want; this is what You want. When my faith is focused on me it is weak, it will grow tired, it will be boring, and it will be empty. But when my faith is focused on God, it is powerful, peaceful, challenging, and alive.

Back to Mindfulness

Mindfulness is pivotal because the way in which we think about what we are doing, has an affect on the impact of our actions. So let's be clear:

- We do not engage in spiritual practices in order to *feel* better.
- We do not engage in spiritual practices in order to *feel* more spiritual.
- We do not engage in spiritual practices because we like them.
- We engage in spiritual practices in order to be more open to God.

This doesn't mean you won't ever feel better or more spiritual (whatever the heck that means) or that you won't like doing them. But if you are engaging in them for any of those purposes, then you are engaging in them with selfish motives. Mindfulness within spiritual practices is not about being *super* attentive; it's about posturing ourselves to accomplish their purpose. Mindfulness is about being aware of what we're doing, opening ourselves up to God.

A new term has become common within "spiritual" conversations. It's not a new term. It's just new to spiritual conversations. The term is self-care. This is a good and important term. To use a common metaphor, before you help the passenger next to you with their oxygen mask, you should put on your own. Jesus continuously retreated to an isolated place to pray and connect with his Heavenly Father. God said to Elijah, "Get up, eat what is in front of you, or the journey ahead will be too much for you." (1 Kings 19:7) Self-care.

But that's not what we mean when we say self-care do we? When we say self-care, we are talking about days off, pedicures, vacations, and abandoning responsibilities to go be by ourselves. True self-care is about ensuring that you are continuously growing as you help others. These things above aren't self-care, they're self-indulgence. It's just a new socially acceptable way of being selfish.

What we have done is dangerously reframe spiritual practices as selfish pursuits. We have taken what was intended to lead to "less of me, more of God" and turned them into "I'm going to take care of me."

If the purpose of your pursuit is to indulge, then it will lead to more indulgence. If the purpose of your pursuit is to be a "great" Christian, then it will only build your ego. If you seek to do something significant for the kingdom and engage in spiritual practices to aid you in this, you will only feed your own desire for significance.

Mindfulness matters.

New Practices

Jesus had a lot to say about this. He tells us to "be careful not to practice your righteousness in front of others to be seen by them." (Matthew 6:1) He doesn't tell us we can't practice our faith in front of others. This is not a statement that everything we do for our faith should be done in secret (how some Christians live). It's a statement that when you're in front of others, make sure you're not doing it for them.

He tells us that when we give, we must not announce it but do it in secret. He tells us when we pray, not to do it with many words as a show to be seen by others but to do it in our rooms, in secret. When we fast, we are not supposed to tell others that we're fasting but only do it before our Heavenly Father. The point is don't do it for others, there will be no reward for that. If you only do it for your Heavenly Father, your reward will be great.

And the reward? That we will become like Him.

So here's my suggestion, my recommendation, and my blueprint. If you want your faith to grow, no matter where it is now—whether you have strong faith, weak faith, no faith— if you have passed through the rigors of deconstruction and have come out stronger on the other side, or if deconstruction has left your once proud faith in a pile of rubble, I believe there is one thing you need to do.

Start practicing your faith without a spotlight on you.

Pray by yourself. Read Scripture, but don't post a pic on Instagram of your Bible next to a cup of coffee. Serve without anyone noticing. Give and don't tell anyone. Meditate on Scripture, even when you don't feel like it. Pray for others, even when you don't like them very much at that moment. Pray for others, but don't tell them (sarcastically or flippantly) that you'll be praying for them. Keep serving, even when you don't feel like it. Even when you're tired. Even when our "self-care" society would tell you to be self-indulgent.

Go to church. Not for you, not for your interests, not for your likes, and not for your preferences. Go to Church for the mission that God has invited you into, which is likely found through the building of his Church and that God will help build within you. Don't just go to church, be the church. Sing in worship, even when you don't know the song, even when you don't like the song, because you're not worshipping you, you're worshipping the Creator of the universe.

Yes, practice self-care. No, do not practice self-indulgence. Because you're not a "come and see" spectator anymore, you're a "go and die" disciple.

Too many of us have made our faith about us. We've obsessed over our own stories and our own personalities. We have a culturally acceptable narcissism, and we wonder why our faith is dying. Faith isn't about us. It's about God. It's not about how we feel; it's about what He's accomplished on our behalf. It's not about what He might give you, but it's about who He is.

We're servants, not spectators. We're servants, not cynics. We're servants of the Most High God. Let's live mindful of that truth.

I want your faith to grow. I believe a faith in Jesus changes absolutely everything. And so it's time that you build again. But differently this time.

CHAPTER THIRTEEN

A NOTE FOR CHRISTIAN LEADERS

To my friends in ministry, fellow pastors, aspiring Christian leaders, and those who are exploring a calling in ministry,

Let's start our conversations here: Deconstructing faith while leading in ministry is a hard thing. The balance of calling people to move forward while simultaneously feeling like our own faith is moving backward is tricky, complex, and can make us feel like imposters at times. We call people to follow God, while we question what following really means.

We read verses about trusting God, we pray for people's trust and faith in God to increase while we wonder how we can trust ourselves.

Then add in the extra layer that, for many of us, this is our livelihood. We pay our mortgages, keep the lights on, and support our families through the financial support provided by the ministries we lead. It's not just the money we make that has created this additional level of complexity; it's the money we've invested. Bachelor's degrees, master's degrees, conferences, trainings. All of these are part of our financial investment to be in full-time ministry. I have friends who carry nearly six digits in school loans and who now question their faith and callings. They find themselves in spots where they have invested everything to be at this moment and in this position, and yet they don't know if they still believe what they're teaching.

There's a verse within all this that kind of haunts us. You know the one. Paul is writing to the Corinthians, again, because they're *still* really, really messed up. He's making the case for why his ministry is different from others'. Why his words should be trusted instead of the false teachers who will let them do whatever they want, so long as they are allowed to stay in positions of authority. He makes the distinction that "we do not peddle the word of God for profit." (2 Cor. 2:17) We do not serve as pastors in order to benefit ourselves, and we're not concerned about our monetary gain.

You certainly didn't enter into ministry to become a peddler of the Gospel. You didn't go through training, education, studies, degrees, internships, and probably volunteered at churches for a countless number of hours to get rich from being in ministry. You're not financially rich. You're just paying your bills. Yet you might still question, "Have I become a peddler of the Gospel?"

You're not alone. There are countless others in ministry who are asking similar questions and going through similar struggles. These people are hard to identify because of the underlying fear that if you confess what you're really struggling with to anyone else they will "tell" on you. Confession to others in ministry and to those we lead in ministry is important but dangerous. Confessing to a spouse or family member can be equally scary. Many people have spouses who define part of their identity on being in ministry or at least have built part of the standard of living upon it. Confessing to whatever authority is over you can be the most terrifying choice to make. While you have built relationships and friendships with these people, you're not quite sure how they will respond. There's the constant fear that confession to someone in authority could be the last conversation you will have while still in full-time ministry.

Does any of this sound familiar? My guess is that this is either your story, you know someone whose story this is, or you are completely isolated within ministry and need to go pick up a copy of *How to Win Friends and Influence People* by Dale Carnegie. So what do you do? How do you navigate it? Do you get out? Do you recommit? Do you go see a counselor? Let's talk about it.

Our Story

I have had a couple of former staff members who deconstructed their faith down to nothing. Some of it was their own doing in pursuit of questions that would certainly lead to the dismantling of their faith. For example, I encouraged one person to read something fun instead of something that was deliberately deconstructive because of where they were personally, and they chose to put Sam Harris aside and read, *The Golden Compass* by Philip Pullman instead. Not exactly a healthy choice in that moment. Some of it was out of their hands, and because of either negative influences from their past or simply a tide of doubt, they could no longer tread water. The point is that I have had several members of my staff leave church because of a lack of faith.

I didn't say I fired them. They left. That distinction is important because if it was the former, you should have no reason to trust my intent within this discussion. You still may not trust me, but I want you to know that I absolutely have your best interest at heart.

They didn't lose/leave their faith and then immediately decide they needed to get out of ministry. No, the process was much more complicated than that. Their acceptance of their lack of faith was paralleled with a willingness to share what they no longer believed in. It was almost as if they couldn't come to grips with the fact that they no longer had faith in God until they verbally processed it with other Christians who they knew cared about them.

Some of these moments were both incredibly interesting and unbelievably tense. One such moment came when our staff was going through a book with a very high Christology and one of our staff members shared how much he disagreed with the author's view. We asked questions and pushed further, as we do with our staff, and eventually he confessed publicly that he really didn't believe that anyone had to know Jesus to go to heaven. He immediately followed that statement up with, "Man, all of a sudden it got really sweaty in here." Everyone nervously looked at me, questioning if this was going to be the end of his employment. It wasn't.

This is what I knew then and still know now:

1. Anytime a pastor is fired, it causes significant damage. Damage to the Church, damage to the people who cared about the pastor, damage to the person himself. Some people will say that churches don't fire enough people, and that may be true. But the more important truth is that when someone loses his or her job from the church, it doesn't feel like they lost a job from the organization, it feels like they lost their job with God.

2. Letting people go from their roles because of struggles, which they confessed, would entirely erode a culture of trust. Trust makes everything easier, better, and quicker. Confession and trust go hand-in-hand. To radically change the course of people's lives because of a doubt they confessed would be the greatest trust-destroying act I can think of.

3. You cannot stay in ministry and not love people, God, and the Church. Ministry is tiring and depleting, and love is the greatest motivator there is. Love is what enables you to get up in the middle of the night to change a diaper. Love is what gives you energy to work out a disagreement. Love motivates like nothing else in the world. So to be in ministry and not love what you are doing and love why you are doing it would eventually be exhausting.

So in each of these scenarios, I took the same approach. I chose to do what was best for the staff members. I talked to them, counseled them, and even debated with them at times. I poked holes in their doubts, I empathized with their struggles of faith, and I helped them find a way forward. But as part of this larger process, I wanted them to see they could no longer stay in full-time ministry. It was not best for the ministry, it was not best for the church, and it would not be best for them either.

So eventually, they transitioned off the staff. They moved on to new careers—some in the non-profit world and some in the business sector. It's what was best for them and our church. If they had stayed on at the church, it would have only caused further damage to their faith, and that's the last thing I wanted.

I received some counsel from ministry friends at the time and have retrospectively shared these accounts, after the fact, with people whom I trust. Some people think I handled it correctly, and some people think I handled it incorrectly. I'm not sure. But I do believe that our first commitment in ministry must parallel the first commitment within the medical community: "First, do no harm." Do no harm to our staff, our churches, to other pastors, or to the community.

I'm constantly reminded that as a leader and a pastor, I always have a greater potential to do harm than good. I can cause more damage to people than create good for them. This doesn't leave me paralyzed in my actions, but it is a sobering reality of what my role is within difficult moments and hopefully, a helpful perspective for those who may be facing this. I obviously want to do the greatest amount of good that I can, but my first responsibility is to do no harm.

Practical Tips If You're In Ministry And Struggling With Deconstruction

Do: Find someone you can talk to about it. It will probably be someone outside your tribe. It may be someone outside ministry. It absolutely could be a Christian counselor. If you are married, it should also be your spouse. Without someone to talk to and process with, the double-life of faith that you feel you are leading will negatively impact your identity in significant ways. Although this is difficult and scary, you can't allow that to happen. Find someone else to go through this with.

Don't: Confess to your church as a whole, especially in a message. The purpose of confessing publicly to others is to benefit the other people. It gives a framework for a relationship to move forward. The purpose of confession, especially for those in leadership, is not to relieve a guilty conscience. When people spill everything in front of everyone, they are damaging others and misusing the platform they have been entrusted with. Instead of using your influence to serve others, you are just using it to serve yourself.

Do: Work through the process of healthy construction as described within this project. Find your anchors; figure out what Jesus believed and not just what you think. Do the difficult work of not just deconstructing your faith but building your faith. Deconstruction has become such a trendy thing that no one seems to realize it's always more difficult to build something than to tear it down.

Don't: Obsess over your questions. Ask your questions, think about your questions, have discussions about your questions, but do not allow them to consume you. Paul tells us, "Take captive every thought." (2 Cor. 10:5) This doesn't mean that as soon as a troubling thought of doubt comes into our heads, we should rid it from of our lives. That is extremely unhealthy. But it is just as unhealthy to allow our minds to be consumed by what troubles us and what we don't know.

Do: Clearly determine the factors keeping you in ministry. Is it a calling you don't want to turn your back on? Or is it financial stress because you don't know what on Earth you would do next? Those are very different reasons for staying in ministry. One is honorable, and the other is understandable but based in fear. Don't deceive yourself because you like the outcome.

Don't: Stay in ministry if you no longer have faith in Jesus. Otherwise, you are the one causing damage, and you are selfishly holding others back, keeping them from stepping into their calling and causing damage to the Church as a whole because of your own fears about moving forward.

During the writing of *Reconstructing the Rubble,* there have recently been several high profile Christian leaders who have publicly declared they are leaving the ministry because they no longer have faith in Jesus. I trust that won't put a time stamp on this work because that is a common phenomenon that seems to continue happening, but it's fresh on my mind.

They have well-stated confessions about their lack of faith, the sources of their doubts, and their decisions to leave the Church and faith for good, all publicly shared for everyone to read. I wonder why they do that. Is it a guilty conscience that tells them they have led everyone astray, and now they need to correct their teachings? Possibly, but it doesn't feel like that.

It feels like they still want to lead.

It feels like they have become so used to the intoxication of a public platform that whether that platform be Christianity or secularism, they want to ensure they still have a public platform.

"Peddlers of the Gospel."

I want your faith to grow. I want you to be healthy. I want you to move forward in your life.

I want to prevent the fear of the new causing you to become stuck in what's now. I want to prevent you from becoming completely exhausted in your life because you're stuck in a ministry and a church that you no longer love. I want to prevent you from becoming so used to your platform that you seek to maintain it regardless of the impact it has on all those around you.

One of the last conversations I had with a staff member whose faith was teetering on the edge was about a message he was preaching. The message was dealing with beliefs that are at the core of Christianity. He told me he was really struggling with the message because he didn't believe it. He couldn't teach something that he didn't believe. I told him, kindly, that people weren't showing up to hear him teach on what he believed. They were there to hear teachings from Scripture. They showed up before him to hear teachings on Scripture, and they would show up after him to hear teachings on Scripture. The teacher is irrelevant in many ways, but the content is central.

We talked about this for a while. We made parallels to a professor who is asked to teach content from a book. Communicating the teacher's unique perspective on the material is not the task. Rather, faithfully teaching the content is what is important.

He decided he couldn't do it anymore. It felt false and inauthentic. So he went to look to do something else.

That was scary, hard, and also courageous. Even in his doubt, he was committed to not hurting the Church, even though he no longer believed in it.

First, do no harm. I hope, if in a similar position, that you would have the same courage. The courage to listen. The courage to care. And the courage to get out if you need to, without attempting to maintain your public platform in the process.

ENDNOTES

Chapter 2

JD Vance, *Hillbilly Elegy: A Memoir of a Family and Culture in Crisis*. New York: Harper, Reprint Edition, 2016.

Chapter 3

Yuval Noah Harari, *Sapiens: A Brief History of Humankind*. New York: Harper, 2015.

JV Chamary, "Is Thanos Right About Overpopulation In 'Avengers: Infinity War?'" *Forbes*, 30 April 2018, https://www.forbes.com/sites/jvchamary/2018/04/30/avengers-infinity-war-overpopulation/#152c31d11c58.

"Killing of Harambe," *Wikipedia,* https://en.wikipedia.org/
wiki/Killing_of_Harambe.

Chapter 4

Vincent Van Gogh, "The Starry Night." 1889, https://www.
vincentvangogh.org/starry-night.jsp.

Makoto Fujimura, "The Starry Night: Biola University
Commencement Address," Makoto Fujimura Blog, 26
May 2012, https://www.makotofujimura.com/writings/
the-starry-night-biola-university-commencement-
address-may-2012/.

John Ortberg, "Ruthlessly Eliminate Hurry," Christianity
Today: Pastors, 4 July 2002, https://www.
christianitytoday.com/pastors/2002/july-online-only/
cln20704.html

Chapter 6

The Arbinger Institute, *Leadership and Self-Deception:
Getting Out of the Box.* San Francisco: Berrett-Koehler
Publishers, Second edition, 2015.

Chapter 9

Rob Bell, *Velvet Elvis: Repainting the Christian Faith.* New
York: HarperOne, Reprint Edition, 2012.

Dietrich Bonhoeffer, *The Cost of Discipleship*. New York:
Touchstone Publishing, 1995.

Chapter 11

"The Apostles' Creed With List of Bible Scripture References," *Access Jesus*, 19 March 2016, http://access-jesus.com/apostles-creed-list-of-bible-refererces-html/.

ABOUT THE AUTHOR

Kevin Jack is passionate about leading people to fulfill their life purposes. He currently serves as the lead pastor of Be Hope Church and podcasts weekly for "Leading Hope with Kevin Jack." He holds a Bachelor's Degree in Religion from MVNU and a Masters in Christian Management and Leadership from Trinity University. He lives in Beavercreek, Ohio with his wife and four children.

CPSIA information can be obtained
at www.ICGtesting.com
Printed in the USA
JSHW041138220321
12783JS00003B/293